I0832380

THE LION'S CUB

WITH OTHER VERSE

BY

RICHARD HENRY STODDARD

NEW YORK
CHARLES SCRIBNER'S SONS
1890

TROW'S
PRINTING AND BOOKBINDING COMPANY,
NEW YORK.

CONTENTS.

PAGE

Liber Amoris, ... 1

Through Darkness, ... 11

The Graves, ... 12

The Door, ... 13

Rich and Poor, ... 13

Succor, ... 14

The Uncreated, ... 15

The Chapter of the Crown, ... 16

The Pilgrimage, ... 17

The Words of Sadi, ... 17

The Bowl, ... 18

The Motherless Child, ... 19

Speech and Silence, ... 20

The Black Camel, ... 20

Rose and Vine, ... 21

He Knows, ... 22

Contents.

PAGE

THE END OF SONG, ... 23

THE BOOKS OF THE SIBYLS, ... 24

THE ROSARY, ... 25

THE NAME, ... 25

THE END, ... 26

THE MORALS OF MARCUS AURELIUS, . . 27

THE POTTER, ... 32

THE DEATH OF MOSES, ... , . 34

THE BRAHMAN'S LESSON, ... 37

MASTER ECKART'S SERMON, ... 41

THE CUP, ... 44

THE WALK AT NIGHT, ... 44

THE ANT, ... 45

LOVERS' HEARTS, ... 46

CLEON AND ÆGLE, ... 47

THE CAPTIVES OF CHARON, ... 47

A LAMENT, ... 49

THE PEARL, ... 50

NO JEWELS, ... 51

CARISSIMA, ... 51

AT DRACHENFELS, ... 52

AT MERRY MOUNT, ... 53

BIRDS OF A FEATHER, ... 54

Contents.

PAGE

Good-night, ... 55

Whence and Whither? 55

The Archetypal Man, ... 58

Four Gazeles of Hafiz, ... 60

The Lady of the East, ... 64

Romances from Gustavo Becquer, . . . 66

Out-of-doors, ... 71

Uncertain Sounds, ... 72

Music, ... 72

A Sailor Song, ... 73

Implora Pacem, ... 74

The Captain's Song, ... 75

To Julia, ... 76

In the Meadows, ... 77

In the Snow, ... 78

How and Why, ... 79

Mors et Vita, ... 80

Thought, ... 81

The Singer, ... 81

A Fantasy, ... 82

Vox Clamantis, ... 83

Children's Songs, ... 84

Father and Child, ... 88

Contents.

PAGE

Our Fathers, ... 91

Thoughts for Thanksgiving, . . . 93

Decoration Day, ... 96

Hair of Washington, ... 99

To Mary Bradley, ... 100

To William James Linton, ... 101

At a Dinner of Artists, ... 102

At Washington, ... 102

Moriturum Salutamus, ... 103

On Nearing the Second Cataract, . . 104

The Crossing of the Ways, ... 104

At Concord, ... 106

At Roslyn, ... 112

The Judgment of Solomon, ... 115

The Legend of Frey Bernardo, . . . 122

The Brahman's Son, ... 132

The Lion's Cub, ... 145

LIBER AMORIS.

I.

UPON the Delphic leaves
Of this prophetic book
Whoever will may look;
No eye but mine perceives
What gladdens there, or grieves,
Nor why the peace of years
Is wrecked with hopes and fears.
Many will read the words,
But none will understand
The meaning, though the birds
Fly up and down the land,
And, wooing, learn and teach
That universal speech.
You know it not, and I
Only so much thereof
As signifies I love—
But not the reason why.

II.

If you see a flower to-day,
  And the scent of it is sweet,
    You will know what it is—
    No flower, but a kiss,
For I blow one your way,
  And it grows at your feet.

If you hear a bird to-day,
  And its melody is dear,
    You will hearken to it long—
    No bird, but a song,
For I wing one your way,
  And it sings in your ear.

If you have my song to-day,
  And you feel its gentle art,
    And if you have my kiss,
    And know how pure it is—
Be careful of them, pray,
  For they are my soul, and heart.

III.

I have rifled land and sea
For similitudes of thee.
First thou wert a Lily, such

As no satyr dares to touch;
Sweetest, purest of all those
That on Dian's couch their snows
Shed, not knowing she is gone
After cold Endymion.
Then I went to Neptune's realm,
Which the waters overwhelm,
Through a light which is not light,
Sinking to the under-night:
There, where Amphitrite's girls
Slumber, pillowed on their curls,
There I sought thee, Pearl of pearls!

Hast thou rifled land and sea
For similitudes of me?
No: for what am I to thee?
Lilies from the first have grown
For no service but their own.
Votaries to themselves they live,
Taking all the heavens give,
Homage of the wind and dew,
Sighs and tears of lovers, too.
Pearls are souls of lilies flown,
Saved because they once were dear,
By the baptism of Love's tear
That turns itself and them to stone.

Since thou hast my sighs and tears,
And the fulness of my years,

No need to rifle land and sea
For poor similitudes of me!

IV.

I sent my darling letters,
  That came of late to me,
Sweet messages from song-birds
  Across the summer sea.

But, if the missives reached her,
  She answered not a word;
My couriers could not meet her,
  This shy and silent bird.

When four dull days were ended,
  Four nights of strange unrest,
There came a little whisper
  From her secluded nest.

She sent me back my letters,
  Which she had kept too long,
And crumpled in their foldings
  Behold a missing song.

I lost it in the letters,
  Of which it seemed a part;
But I lost much more than that there—
  I lost with that my heart!

V.

What does she think of me? I ask myself,
Who am not ignorant what I think of her.
She thinks I am too old, and she too young
(She Spring, I Autumn), or thinks not at all.
It may be, *must* be, for she sends no word
That words of mine have reached her. Be it so.
If of herself she does not love me—well.
She need not fear that I shall sue to her.
I am too old for that, and she too young;
But youth like hers (dear youth!) and age like mine—
Did not old Goethe love the young Bettina,
And did not young Bettina love old Goethe?

VI.

Why do I love you—if I do?
Tell me that, and I'll tell you.
It is not that you are more fair
Than other ladies whom I know;
For the summer of your hair,
Or the lights that come and go
In your radiant, startled eyes,
Apprehensive of surprise;
Nothing in your bright, young face,
Which is comely, I suppose;

No illusive charm, or grace;
What it is, Heaven only knows.
I might not love you if I knew,
For what I love might not be you!

VII.

When woman loves, and will not show it,
    What can her lover do?
I asked a scholar, and a poet,
But neither wise fool seemed to know it;
    So, lady, I ask you.

Were you in love—let me suppose it—
    What should your lover do?
You know you love him, and he knows it;
Oh, why not, then, to him disclose it,
    As he his love to you?

VIII.

Thrice have I spoken, and from you no sign
That my poor words have reached you. They *are*
    poor,
Or you would not have shut your spirit's door,
But would have opened it to words of mine.
What is there in me, tell me, and my line,
Yours, also, who are poet, that no more
You greet us kindly as you did before?
Because that we are human, you divine?

Am I too old to love you? Or do you
Love some one younger better? Be it so:
Whatever happens I am still your friend.
You may have hurt me somewhat, let it go;
I shall live down my weakness, poets do,
And have, like stronger men, a peaceful end.

IX.

This man loves me. If you have ever said
These woman's words, it was to yourself alone;
But you have never said them, never known
The difference between my heart and head.
The songs that I have written you have read
As shallow fancies, which your way have flown;
You have not felt there the deep undertone
Where what still lives in me laments its dead.
But you will feel it when the busy hand
That pens this fervent page hath lost its skill;
And when the heart that urges it is still
And cold as yours, then you will understand
My pure and strong devotion, and will be
Constrained to say, too late: This man loved me.

X.

Needless was your command
  To burn your letters:
Nor woman's heart, nor hand,
  Hold I in fetters.

Be your weak vows forgot,
  My vow is stronger;
No : since you trust me not,
  You love no longer.

Go, lightly, as ye came,
  Perish, each letter ;
Why not, since in the flame
  I read them better ?

XI.

If we had never met, dear,
  Would we have loved as now ?
Or lived in vain regret, dear,
  Apart, we know not how ?

I cannot understand, dear,
  The riddle of my life ;
Why *he* has now your hand, dear,
  And you are not my wife.

If hearts are wed by fate, dear,
  And ordered things befall,
Why did we meet too late, dear ?
  Why did we meet at all ?

XII.

The immortal part of me,
If any such there be,
Doth still in me remain ;
I know it by my pain,
And by my love for thee :

Only for this I would be dust,
As soon, proud one, I must.
Soften, O Love, that heart of hers,
So hard to all her worshippers,
So doubly hard to me.

See, where thy lover stands,
And stretches forth his hands ;
His supplications hear,
Dying because thou art too dear.
Come near,
And, giving nothing else, O, give him now a tear.

XIII.

In the stillness of night,
In the chill moonlight,
What is it that I hear,
Coming near, near, near?

I peer in the darkness, but nothing I see,
Though a shadow is falling,
And voices are calling,
Half pain, half delight:
Art thou sighing for me?
Am I dying for thee?
Alone, all alone in the night!

Ah, no, no, no,
For the voices go,
And a burst of music comes,
The trumpet blows a blast,
And the cymbals follow fast,
With the rattle and the roll of the
drums.
The night is past; the morn is here at last,
And a ship is sailing in, with my colors at her
mast.
My lady at the prow,
Like a Queen upon her throne,
Waves her hand to me now,
And my sorrow is flown.
It was she who was sighing
Till the land came in sight,
For she feared I was dying
In the watches of the night,
Alone, all alone in the night!

THROUGH DARKNESS.

ONE night the Angel Gabriel,
  Seated in Paradise apart,
Heard the low, loving Voice of God
  In answer to a human heart.

"Eminent must this servant be,
  Who to the Most High is so nigh;
Whose spirit, dead to lust below,
  Already is with Him on high."

He hastened over land and sea
  To find this man—he went like light;
But found him not, in earth or Heaven,
  Through all the watches of the night.

"O Lord, direct me to this man,
  That is so near and dear to Thee."
"The man thou speakest of, Gabriel,
  Thou shalt in yon pagoda see."

Straightway to the pagoda sped
  The Instructed One, and, looking there,
Beheld before an idol grim
  A solitary man in prayer.

Rich and Poor.

THE DOOR.

(*Jelaluddin.*)

ONE knocked at the Beloved's door.
"Who is there?" The loud reply
  To the Voice within was, "I."
"Go thy ways and come no more,
  This house holds not Me and Thee;
  Who himself loves, loves not Me."
Closed was the Beloved's door.

Back to the Beloved's door,
  After twelve months' prayer and fast,
  In the desert lone and vast,
The lover came and knocked once more.
  "Who is there?" the answer now
  Was no longer "I," but "Thou."
Opened was the Heavenly Door.

RICH AND POOR.

SEATED beside his father's tomb
  I saw a rich man's son one day,
  Who speaking with a poor man's son
  Reproved him, in his lordly way.

THE DOOR.

(*Jelaluddin.*)

ONE knocked at the Beloved's door.
"Who is there?" The loud reply
  To the Voice within was, "I."
"Go thy ways and come no more,
  This house holds not Me and Thee;
  Who himself loves, loves not Me."
Closed was the Beloved's door.

Back to the Beloved's door,
  After twelve months' prayer and fast,
  In the desert lone and vast,
The lover came and knocked once more.
  "Who is there?" the answer now
  Was no longer "I," but "Thou."
Opened was the Heavenly Door.

RICH AND POOR.

SEATED beside his father's tomb
  I saw a rich man's son one day,
Who speaking with a poor man's son
  Reproved him, in his lordly way.

Succor.

"My father's tomb of marble is,
  Costly and beauteous to behold;
And lo, on alabaster graved
  His name in characters of gold.

What likeness to thy father's tomb
  Has it, as high as that is low?
Builded of brick, with dust thereon,
  Not more than Summer winds might blow."

"Peace," said the poor man's son. "Before
  The heavy stone that on him lies
Thy father shall have moved a jot,
  Mine will have entered Paradise.

'Hear, rich and poor,' the Prophet saith:
  'And choose ye straightway which is best,
Earth, which rich men disquiet so,
  Or Heaven, which is the poor man's rest.'"

SUCCOR.

BENEATH a shady tree, alone,
Far from his camp, Mohammed slept,
When on his slumbers, sword in hand,
Darther, a hostile warrior, crept.
"Awake, Mohammed!" shouted he;
"Who is there that can succor thee?"

Mohammed answered him: "The Lord;"
Whereat the chief let fall the sword.

The Prophet snatched the sword, and said:
"Thou seest that God hath succored me:
If I should smite thee, Darther, now;
Who is there that could succor thee?"
"Alas, not one." "Then learn of me
The mercy I extend to thee.
Take back thy sword." The legend ends.
Be sure from that day they were friends.

THE UNCREATED.

(*Arabic.*)

"WHERE, Allah, shall I find thee?"
    And answered all around:
"Know that when thou hast sought Him
    Thou hast already found."

"How knoweth thou Allah liveth?"
    They asked a Bedouin;
"What! Does this dawn need torchlight
    In order to be seen?"

Ascend the highest Heaven,
  Still Allah is above;

Not reached, but comprehended
  By his eternal Love.

Words that are worthy of Him
  Have never yet been heard.
Let us adore in silence
  The Uncreated Word.

THE CHAPTER OF THE CROWN.

WHAT are the words of Allah
  In the Chapter of the Crown?
"In the night of Al Kadr
  We sent the Koran down.
How shalt thou understand it,
  That dost so little know
How excellent that night is,
  And how its watches go?
That holy night is better
  Than a thousand moons of years;
For then descend the angels,
  And Gabriel appears
By the command of Allah,
  Whose just decrees they bear
Concerning every creature
  That Death shall smite, or spare.

Peace till the morning rises
  In tent, and tower, and town;
For in the night of Al Kadr
  We sent the Koran down."

THE PILGRIMAGE.

FOOTSORE, behind the caravan
That went to Mecca, Rabia crept,
Until at the Kaaba they began
Their prayers to offer; then she wept,
And beat her breast. "What dost thou seek,
O heart, weak follower of the weak?
Thou hast traversed land and sea,
And the burning desert trod,
To find in this far place the God
That long ago had come to thee."

THE WORDS OF SADI.

REFLECT upon the words that Sadi penned.
Reveal not every secret to a friend:
For how can you foretell what is to be?
He may, hereafter, be your enemy.
And with your enemy the wisest plan
Is not to do him all the harm you can;

For it may happen to you in the end
To make your present enemy a friend.
The hand that can withhold, the tongue discreet,
These fit the Sheik to fill the Sultan's seat.

THE BOWL.

(*Attar.*)

TRAVELLING in a desert land,
  I saw a spring at my feet :
Into the waters I dipped my hand—
  Was never water so sweet !

Passing on I was wild to sing,
  I rejoiced so in my soul.
Another traveller came to the spring,
  And drank from an earthen bowl.

He departs, and leaves his bowl behind,
Which I, returning, straightway find ;
But the bubbling spring is sweet no more—
Was never water so bitter before.

Then a Voice through me like a shudder ran :
" That Bowl was moulded out of Man,
Who cannot (as the Prophet saith),
Lose the bitter flavor of Death ! "

THE MOTHERLESS CHILD.

(Arabic.)

TAKE thy way to the grave,
  Where lies thy lost and dear;
Lift up thy voice and cry—
  Ah, if she could but hear!

Why hast thou gone to dwell
  In that far land apart,
Whereto the valiantest
  Go with a quaking heart?

That place of lonesome shade
  Is most unmeet for thee;
God's love be with thee there,
  His pity be with me.

The little one thou hast left,
  God pity her—for she
Knows not what she has lost;
  And yet she weeps for thee.

Those dear, sweet ways of thine
  She misses make her weep;
We hush her all night long,
  But the poor child cannot sleep.

When her crying in the night
  Smites on my sleepless ears,
Straightway mine eyes are filled,
  From the well of bitter tears.

SPEECH AND SILENCE.

WHAT'S spoken here none discloses;
  Gone, like a breath, out of reach
  Are the free, light words of each:
Our mouths are silent roses
  About our budding speech.

I am the bard of the roses,
  You, sweet one, are the dew,
  Slipped out of heaven's blue,
Where Love, on his bed reposes,
  Dreaming, dear heart, of you.

THE BLACK CAMEL.

FULL-BLOWN are the royal roses,
  And ripe are the grapes on the vines;
For the Sun in his high pavilion,
  The Sultan of summer, shines.

Rose and Vine.

The world is the garden of Irem,
  Or would be, with one thing more—
The absence of Death's black camel,
  That is kneeling at every door.

ROSE AND VINE.

If you hearken to me,
Be it as one who knows
There is life in the wind he breathes,
Though he sees not whence it blows,
Nor whither, at last, it goes.
What I say to-day,
To-morrow I may unsay.
I saw a thorn last night,
This morning it is a Rose.

If I hearken to you
It is in the same large way;
The words may be yours, or mine:
If the cup be filled with wine,
Who cares if the cup be clay?
No man knows
Where the Vine grows,
Or whence the scent
In the heart of the Rose.
We know all we need to know
Since they are ours to-day.

HE KNOWS.

THE temple that I frequent most,
Has, for its dome, the turquoise sky,
On unseen pillars lifted up.
I sell my holy rosary
Strung with His Names, nor count it lost,
So that it gains enough to buy
The Wine that fills Creation's Cup.

I turn—such might to me belongs—
Austerest prayers to sweetest songs ;
I make—such spells I cast around—
The whole, wide world enchanted ground.
Wisdom Supreme, the Earth is thine,
The Cup, whereof Thou art the Wine,
The light, the shade that ebbs and flows,
Whatever comes, whatever goes,
All things begin and end in Thee.
Whence leads the path of destiny?
I know not. But He knows—He knows.

THE END OF SONG.

(*Jami.*)

"I SANG when I was young,
  Ah, me, how merrily then.
I captured the notes of birds,
  I won the hearts of men.

My singing days are done:
  Why should an old man sing?
Why hover about a nest,
  When the birds have taken wing?

They go, and come not back;
  It is a hint, I see,
That I have stayed too long,
  And men are tired of me."

These were the words of Jami, who
Still sang, as poets wont to do,
Songs against singing. Critics say
That Jami is alive to-day.

THE BOOKS OF THE SIBYLS.

WHERE are the books of the Sibyls
  The high gods sent to men,
Writ upon leaves of marble
  With what Eternal Pen?

The wise Cumæan Sibyl
  Had not destroyed a line
Of those she brought to Tarquin,
  The three that once were nine,

If the Powers had been propitious,
  And the reign of peace was near;
But the words were of swords—not
    ploughshares,
  And the prophecy austere.

Gone are the books of the Sibyls,
  Sent down to earth in vain;
But others still more dolorous
  In the soul of Man remain.

THE ROSARY.

I HOLD not one, but many creeds;
I am the string, and they the beads.
What Buddha felt, and Plato thought,
And Jesus and Mohammed taught,
I know; not what it is to Thee,
Thou Maker of the Rosary!

THE NAME.

A SPIRIT was with me in sleep,
  And in my fingers placed a pen:
What was commanded me I wrote,
  His message to the sons of men.

"Before the beginning was, I am;
  And I after the end shall be;
Unseen behind the loom of Time
  Weaving the web, Eternity.

My feet are on the mountain-tops,
  And in the hollows of the sea;
To seek Me is to miss Me there,
  To miss is to discover Me.

The constellations rise and set
  At their appointed hours in space,
But see Me not ; their lord, the Sun,
  Hath never looked upon my Face."

But we, if we behold Thee not,
  Are torches lighted at Thy flame ;
For lo, our souls are letters in
  The Incommunicable Name.

THE END.

TELL me, what does it mean ?
  That thou hast reached the end,
Hast gone on board, the voyage made,
  And come to shore ? Descend.

If to another life,
  As wisest men declare,
There is be sure no want of gods—
  They follow even there.

If haply to a state
  That knows no joy nor pain,
Thou wilt no longer tug the oar
  Nor make the voyage again.

THE MORALS OF MARCUS AURELIUS

Humanest of the Roman Race,
As thoughtful as thou wert benign,
If what thou wert be living yet,
It must be in a sacred Place.
Accept, then, with a gracious face,
Great Soul, in these poor words of mine,
A portion of the mighty debt
I owe thee, wisest of thy line :
MARCUS AURELIUS ANTONINE.

I.

THERE is one end, and only one,
  For all the sons of men ;
All Life drifts that way, once begun,
As rivers to the ocean run.
  Remember this, and when
Following the millions gone before,
  Thy voyage, or long, or short, is made,
  Be not disheartened, nor afraid—
For thou art come to shore.
If Life continue there to be,
  And why not there as here ?
Powers will be there protecting thee,
  To whom good deeds are dear.

But if Life be not there, and then,
Thou art no worse off than greater men--
Than is the sage Hippocrates,
Who could not cure his own disease ;
Than Pompeius, Caius Cæsar are,
Who wrapt the lands in clouds of war,
And added to their dark renown
By burning conquered cities down,
And in whose battles, won in vain,
The earth was cumbered with the slain
Of cavalry and infantry ;
They like the meanest had to die.
Accept the end, then, since thou must,
And if thou nothing art but dust,
'Tis something to lay down the oar,
And feel thou shall not labor more.

II.

Who has a vehement desire
  For fame when dead, considers not
That all who may remember him
  Will die, like him, and be forgot ;
And also they who follow them,
  Till all remembrances of fame
  Like torches are, that once were flame,
But now, gone out, in ashes lie.
  Lighting no more the paths of men,
Who foolishly admire, and die.

But say that they immortal are,
  And say that fame immortal be,
When thou art, as thou will be—dust,
  Pray, how will that advantage thee ?

III.

Observe the little one-day fly
  That spreads its summer wings :
So transient is the life of earth,
  So worthless human things.

What yesterday was seed of man
  To-day is man in turn,
To-morrow will a mummy be,
  Or ashes, in an urn.

Pass through this little space of time
  The gods have kindly lent,
And, living naturally, end
  Thy journey in content ;

Just as an olive when it falls,
  Dead ripe with sun and dew,
Thanking the power that brought it forth,
  And the tree whereon it grew.

IV.

The Universe is ebb and flow ;
All things are hurrying to and fro,

Some into life, some out again;
Nothing doth permanent remain,
For even of that which now comes on
A portion is already gone.
In this ever-flowing stream
Of things which are, and things which seem,
Where there is no abiding,
No barque at anchor riding,
What is there that goes fleeting by,
Lust of the flesh, or pride of the eye,
That a man should set his heart upon?
It is just as if he should fall in love
With one of the sparrows above,
Which, while he watches its flight,
Already has passed out of sight.

V.

Let all the good thou dost to man
  A gift be, not a debt;
And he will more remember thee
  The more thou dost forget.

Do it as one who knows it not,
  But rather like a vine,
That year by year brings forth its grapes,
  And cares not for the wine.

A horse, when he has run his race,
  A dog, when tracked the game,

A bee, when it has honey made—
  Do not their deeds proclaim.

Be silent, then, and, like the vine,
  Bring forth what is in thee;
It is thy duty to be good,
  And man's to honor thee.

VI.

If the gods have determined life for me,
They have determined well; for, without forethought,
It is not easy to imagine gods.
As to their harming me—why should they harm me?
Pray what advantage would that be to them,
Or to the whole, whereof I am a part,
Which is the object of their providence?
If they have not determined life for me,
They surely have determined for the whole,
And what comes to me as a part of that,
I should accept, with pleasure and content.
But if they have determined about nothing—
Which I, for one, hold wicked to believe;
Or, if we do believe it, let us not
Make sacrifice, or pray, or swear by them,
Or do aught reverential that we do,
As if the gods were here, and lived with us:

But if, however, they determine nothing,
I can and will determine for myself;
At least, I will search into what is good;
And what is good for one is good for all.
My mind is rational, companionable,
My city and my country (ruling both)
So far as I am Antonine, is Rome;
So far as I am man, is the whole world.

THE POTTER.

I WATCHED a potter at his wheel one day,
For he was making pitchers out of clay,
  The feet of beggars and the heads of kings,
Dust blown from old, dead cities far away.

Not Heaven itself more splendid is and high
Than was this palace, when its kings went by,
  Race after race. The turtle sits here now.
"Where? where?" she cries. But there is no reply.

They who endowed with wisdom are like light,
Torches to guide their followers' feet aright,
  They have not taken yet one step beyond
This night of mystery—this awful Night.

Speak of these wise ones, then, with bated breath ;
The most that of the wisest Wisdom saith,
  Is—they bequeathed you fables, nothing more,
Before returning to the sleep of death.

The great wheel of the Heavens will still go round,
When you and I, my friend, are underground ;
  At once creating life, conspiring death,
With Death and Life inexorably bound.

Come, sit upon the grass, and drink your wine,
And quickly while the suns of summer shine ;
  For other grass than that you sit upon
Will soon be springing from your dust and mine.

When you and I are gone, for we must go,
They will raise bricks above us, and I know
  That other bricks for other tombs than ours
Will out of us be moulded. Be it so.

I do not fear the world. I do not fear
The leaving it, though I confess it dear.
  We should fear nothing but not living well,
In the only life and world we know of—*Here.*

But come, my friend, since we must pass away,
Since all we are goes back again to clay,
  What does it matter whether we remain
A hundred years, or but a single day ?

Be it our care, since pitchers we began,
To hold the heart's good wine long as we can,
  Before the potter moulds our dust again
Into new shapes that are no longer *Man.*

THE DEATH OF MOSES.

NOW Moses knew his hour of death was nigh ;
For the Most High commanded Sammael
To fetch His servant's soul to Paradise—
Sammael, who, clothed in anger, grasped his sword
To slay him, and would have slain, but for the light
Wherewith his face shone, while his hand went on
Writing the Incommunicable Name.
"What ails thee, Moses? Why art thou so pale?
What evil hath befallen us?" Zipporah asked.
And Moses said : "My hour of death is come!"
"What! must a man who hath spoken with God die thus?
Thou, like a common man?" "I must, all must,
The angels Michael, Gabriel, Israfel,
God only is eternal, and dies not.
Where are my children?" "They are put to sleep."
"Wake them ; for I must say farewell to them."

Beside the children's bed she wept and moaned;
" Wake, rise, and bid your father now farewell,
Orphans! for this is his last day on earth!"
They woke in terror. "Who will pity us
When we are fatherless?" "Who will pity them
When they are fatherless?" And Moses wept.
Then God spake to him: "Dost thou fear to die?
Or dost thou leave this earth reluctantly?"
And Moses said: "I do not fear to die,
Nor do I leave this earth reluctantly.
But I lament these children of mine age,
Who have their grandsire and their uncle lost,
And who will lose their father, if I die."
"In whom did she, thy mother, then confide,
When thou by her wast in the bulrush ark
Committed to the Nile?" "In Thee, O Lord!"
"Who hardened Pharaoh's heart, and gave thee
power
Before him and his gods, and to thy hand
A staff to part the waters?" "Thou, O Lord!"
"And fearest to trust thy children unto Me,
Who am the Father of the Fatherless?
Go; take thy staff and over the sea once more
Extend it, and thou shalt behold a sign
To strengthen thy weak faith." And he obeyed.
He took the rod of God, and, going down
To the desolate sea-beach, he stretched it there.
The sea divided, as when clouds are driven
Along the path of a whirlwind, and he saw

A black rock in it, whereunto he went;
And reaching soon the rock, a voice cried,
"Smite!"
He smote; it clave asunder, and therein,
At its foundation was a little cleft,
And in that cleft, with a green leaf in its mouth,
A worm, which lifting up its voice, cried thrice,
"Praise be to God, who hath not forgotten me,
Worm that I am, in holy darkness here!
Praise be to Him, who cherishes even me!"
When the low voice was silent, heard of all
The angels in the pauses of their hymn,
For they ceased singing to behold that sign
Of God's exceeding love—He spake again:
"Thou seest that I consider and provide
Not for man only, but for a little worm,
In a rock whereof men know not, in the waves,
Far in the dark depths of the barren sea.
Shall I forget thy children who know Me?"
Then Moses, so instructed of the Lord,
Comforted his children and his sorrowing wife;
And, leaning on his staff, went forth alone,
To climb the mountain where he was to die;
And where, when he had closed his weary eyes,
And pressed his hand upon his pulseless heart,
God kissed His servant, and he was with Him.

THE BRAHMAN'S LESSON.

ONE summer day a farmer and his son
Were working wearily in the harvest-field.
It was a lonesome place, and dangerous;
For now was come the season of the snakes,
Whereof the deadliest, a great, hooded Thing,
Did sting the young man so that suddenly
He died, for remedy in plant, or herb,
Medicinal root, or skill of leech, is none
Against the venom of that dreadful death,
That darkens the eyes at noonday as with night,
And chills the blood in the heart that beats no more.
This happened; and the father saw his son,
Struck out of life so early, lie there dead,
And saw the gathering of the hungry ants,
Nor sighed, nor ceased a moment from his work.
But now a Brahman chanced to pass that way,
And saw all this, but understood it not.
"Who is that man there dead?" "He was my son."
"Thy son? Why dost thou not lament him, then?
Hast thou no love, nor sorrow for the dead?"
"And wherefore sorrow? From the first bright hour
When he is born, even to his last dark day,

Man's steps are deathward; everything he does
Sets ever that way; there is no escape.
For the well-doing there is recompense,
And for the wicked there is punishment.
Of what avail, when they are gone, are tears?
They can in nowise help us, or the dead.
But thou canst help me, Brahman, if thou wilt.
Go straightway to my house, and tell my wife
What hath befallen—that my son is dead;
And tell her to prepare my noonday meal."
"What manner of man is this?" the Brahman
thought,
Indignantly: "Insensate, ignorant, blind,
He has no human feeling, has no heart."
So thinking, he drew near the farmer's house,
And called his wife: "Woman, thy son is dead.
Thy husband bade me tell thee this: and add
That he is ready for his noonday meal."
The dead man's mother harkened to his words
As calmly as the sky to winds or waves.
"That son received a passing life from us,
From that old man, his father, and from me,
His mother, but I called him not my son.
He was a traveller halting at an inn,
Of which the master entertains the guests,
But not detains. He rested and passed on.
So is it, sir, with mothers, and with sons.
Why, then, should I lament what was to be?"
Still wondering, the troubled Brahman turned

To where the sister of the dead man was,
Bright in the lotus bloom of womanhood.
"Thy brother is dead. Hast thou no tears for
 him?"
She harkened gravely, as the forest doth
To the low murmur of the populous leaves.
"Sometimes," she said, "a stalwart woodman
 goes,
And with his mighty axe hews down the trees,
And binds them fast together in a raft,
And in a seaward river launches them.
Anon the wild wind rises, and the waves,
Lashed in tumultuous warfare, dash the raft
Hither and thither, till it breaks asunder,
And the swift current, separating all,
Whirls all on ruinous shores, to meet no more,
Such, and no other, was my brother's fate.
Why, then, should I lament what was to be?"
Wondering still more, for still the awfulness
Of death, which they perceived not, was to him
As palpable as his shadow on the wall,
The Brahman addressed him to the dead man's
 wife:
"And thou, upon whose loving breast he lay,
Heart answering heart, with lips that breathed in
 sleep
Remembrance of endearments without end,
What wilt thou do without him day and night?"
She harkened tenderly, as the summer noon

To the continuous cooing of the doves ;
" As when two birds, that fly from distant lands,
One from the East, the other from the South—
They meet, and look into each other's eyes,
And, circling round each other, bill to bill,
Seek the same nest, on temple roof, or tree,
And rest together till the dawn is come:
Such was my husband's happy life, and mine.
Was, but is not ; for, as when morning breaks,
Awakened, the coupled birds forsake the nest,
And fly in opposite ways to seek their food ;
They, if it be their destiny, meet no more.
Why, then, should I lament what was to be ? "
Silenced by their submission, which was wise,
Whether the foolish heart think so or not,
The Brahman watched the women in the house,
As to and fro their slender figures moved
Athwart the sunlight streaming through the door,
While they prepared the farmer's noonday meal,
And, watching them, was comforted to learn
The simple secret of their cheerful faith,
That Death the natural sequence is of Life,
And no more dreadful in itself than Life.

MASTER ECKART'S SERMON.

(*Strassburg*, 1320.)

"HEAR Doctor Eckart, hear him!" he began:
"There was in days of old a learned man,
Who longing for the truth eight years did pray
That God would show him some one who the way
Thereto would show. And on a time, when he
Was in great longing and perplexity,
He heard a voice from heaven, or in his mind:
'Go to the front of the church, where thou wilt find
One that the way to blessedness will show.'
Thither he went as fast as he could go,
And found a man whose clothes to rags were worn,
Whose bare and dusty feet were bruised and torn,
Who looked like one acquainted long with sorrow.
He greeted him with—'God give you good-morrow.'
'I never had ill-morrow.' Then said he,
Wondering at what he heard, 'God prosper thee.'
'I never had aught but prosperity.'
'Heaven save you,' said the scholar. He again:
'Other than saved I never was.' 'Explain;
I understand not.' 'Willingly,' said the man,
Whose thoughts upon their conversation ran:
'Thou wishest me good-morrow; I reply,
I never had ill-morrow; for am I

Hungry or thirsty, I praise God ; or, say
That I am shivering, as I am to-day—
Fair or foul weather—hail, or snow, or rain—
As I praised God before, I do again.
Thence comes it that I never had ill-morrow.
And thou didst say, as if I was in sorrow,
God prosper thee, poor man ! I answer thus :
Sir, I have never been unprosperous :
For I know how to live with God, and know
That what He does is best, and make it so ;
Pleasure or pain, whatever may befall,
I take it cheerfully, as best of all,
And so I never had adversity.
God bless thee, then saidst thou ; and I to thee—
I never was unblessed. I long to be
Only of God's will ; to the Will Divine
I have so given what once was will of mine
That what God wills, I will, and all is well.'
' But if God were to cast thee into Hell,
What wouldst thou then ? ' the scholar asked. And
he :
' God cast me into Hell ? It could not be ;
His goodness holds Him back. But, if not so,
I have two arms that would not let Him go :
One is Humility, and therewith I
Would straight take hold of His humanity ;
And with the other, that lifts me above
Up to his Godhead, the right arm of Love,
I would embrace Him till He came to me,

And happier there with Him my soul would be
Than in the Heavens without Him!' Thereupon
The scholar mused, and understood anon
That not the high and learned path he trod,
But one much lower, nearest was to God.
'Whence comest thou?' he asked. 'From God.'
'And where
Hast thou found God?' 'Where I abandoned
care—
Where I abandoned all. I am a king;
My kingdom is my soul, and everything,
Within, without, of which I have control—
All that I am does homage to my soul;
No kingdom on the earth so great as this.'
'And what hath brought thee to such perfect
bliss?'
'Silence, and thought—a mind with God pos-
sessed,
Resolved in nothing less than God to rest:
I have found God—what more the Seraphim?
And everlasting rest and joy in him.'"

So Master Eckart spake, and went his way,
And many wondered, as they do to-day.

THE CUP.

COME, fill the goblet up,
  And pass the rosy wine ;
I will not take the cup
  From any hand but thine.

It is not merely wine
  That thou dost pour for me ;
But something more divine
  That is bestowed by thee.

Though water fill the skin,
  The draught should still be mine :
For thou wouldst look therein,
  And make the water—wine.

THE WALK AT NIGHT.

TELL me what is sweeter
  Than a walk at night,
With one we love beside us
  And the moon in sight ?

Who would have thought the Spring-time
  So prodigal could be ?
Behold the blossoms burning,
  Like lamps on every tree.

The Ant.

What tree is this? An almond?
  A peach, it seems to me;
And the fruit there—pluck it darling,
  The heart I offer thee.

THE ANT.

GO to the ant, thou sluggard,
  Consider all her ways,
And thou shalt be instructed
  To live contented days.

Not like those fools of summer,
  The wasp and dragon-fly,
That flaunt their gaudy garments
  For one short hour, and die.

But, clad in sober sables,
  She goes upon her way,
A busy, little housewife,
  Whose life is work, not play.

She heeds not sun nor shadow,
  She knows not waste nor want,
But prudent is, like Nature
  That loves the prosperous ant.

LOVERS' HEARTS.

(*Servian.*)

FULL of wine, two branches of a vine
  To the walls of Buda clung ;
But no, they were not branches full of wine—
  They were lovers, fair and young.
Happy both, and bound in tender troth,
  They were rudely torn apart ;
Dreadful was the dolor fell on both—
  Ruined hope and broken heart !
(Though those lovers now are dead,
This is what their spirits said) :

"There's a rose that in love's garden grows,
  Sweeter, redder than the rest ;
Go, and pluck, and wear that royal rose
  On thy heart and in thy breast ;
Watch it, and as its petals drop apart,
Remember so my heart dies in thy heart ! "

" Bright as gold, a shaft of marble cold
  Rises where love's fountains flow ;
And on that shaft there is a cup of gold.
  And the cup is full of snow ;
With thy whiter hand take up
All the snow from out that cup,

And, like a bird within its nest,
On my heart, and in my breast,
Softly lay the snow, and say :
As it melts in tears away,
So his hopes of life depart,
For so my broken heart dies in thy heart ! "

CLEON AND ÆGLE.

A DEAR young Greek girl long ago
Went dreaming to a portico,
And sent abroad her thoughts of love ;
When lo, from somewhere came a dove,
And took the letter she had writ
(Scoff not graybeard, to show thy wit),
To her lover Cleon, who received,
And to his dying day believed
It was no dove with silken fetter
But Ægle's Heart that bore the Letter !

THE CAPTIVES OF CHARON.

(*Romaic.*)

ALONG the gloomy hills,
  Where the winds of winter blow,
I see the awful shadow
  Of Charon come and go.

The Captives of Charon.

Before him he drives the young,
  Behind he drags the old,
And, seated on his saddle,
  The children he doth hold.

The old men come and pray,
  Their hands the young men wring,
"O halt beside some village,
  Beside some flowing spring!

That the old may quench their thirst,
  The young the discus throw,
And the children gather flowers
  That on the margin grow."

But Charon shakes his head,
  And hurries on the way;
"I halt beside no village,
  And by no spring I stay.

For mothers coming there
  Would know the babes they bore,
And their late-lost wives the husbands—
  And none could part them more."

So Charon over the hills,
  With swift and silent tread,
Upon his black horse mounted
  Compels the Captive Dead!

A LAMENT.

(Japanese.)

FIVE long, dreary years have fled
Since I saw my lover dead,
And never once since that dark hour
Have my fingers had the power
To loosen his girdle from my breast,
Where nevermore will lover rest.

Before my cottage, poor and low,
Pinks, which are Love's buds, I sow,
But the poor things will not grow.
Barrenly stretch the marshes long,
All over which, so shrill and strong,
Rises the desolate cormorant's song.
But is it the cormorant I hear,
That, just now distant, now is near?
And sudden rain from the autumn skies,
That so bedims my weary eyes?
Ah no: it is the tears I shed,
And my lamentation for the dead!

THE PEARL.

(*Japanese.*)

THE maple lifts her head,
Crowned with autumnal red,
Where I, who love the girl,
Plunge for the biggest pearl,
Down under the deep waves,
And round the hollow caves,
Where angry waters whirl.

"Wert thou a pearl," she cried,
" I would clasp thee on my arm,
To protect me like a charm
From all the world beside.
I give my heart to thee,
Do thou give thine to me ;
Be this the hour and place,
For on my lonely bed,
With the bride-wreath on my head,
I wait for thy embrace."

NO JEWELS.

(Hafiz.)

No tire-woman here is needed
  To clothe thy body, Dear!
The tip of a woman's finger,
  And the small shell of her ear,
Require no precious jewels,
  Nor no such thing
  As a turquoise ring.
  Her loveliness is clear,
  All that it lacks is a smile—
    Perhaps a tear!

CARISSIMA.

Or ever you came weeping,
Your lonely vigil keeping,
Where the dust of Love is sleeping,
    Machree!
Like a wood-mouse softly creeping,
Where the pale moonshine is sweeping
    The locks of the sea,
    For you, dear, and me.

Your Patrick will love you,
Till the great Day above you
Has plunged into Night;
Till the sea is drained dry
By the sip of a fly,
Till the dead are alive, and the far is the nigh;
In the kingdom of light,
Let me die at your feet,
Nora, sweet!

AT DRACHENFELS.

ALL simple folk, like dogs and children dear,
Are experts in the language of the eyes;
The spirit that behind the letter lies
To their sharp sense is clear,
And the words that are unspoken they can hear.
Then why not I and you?
We love, or think we do,
While the river rushes by,
And the summer sky is blue.
Then fill our cups with wine,
I, yours, and you, mine.
For long before all these,
Whatever be their shapes,
Before the wine the grapes,
And before the grapes the vine,

Where it sparkles in the showers, and dances in
the breeze,
Was your love and mine!
Such, dear, as I surmise,
Is the verdict of your eyes,
As we stroll this summer noon, by the many-
castled Rhine.

AT MERRY MOUNT.

OH, what is the use now of sighing,
When any or all things go wrong?
Why question, when there's no replying?
Much better go sing an old song.
Leave to women repining and dying,
A man should be merry and strong,
The worst, when it comes, is but dying,
And the longest of lives is not long.
Sing, "Care hanged a cat,
And Sorrow drowned a rat,
But a cavalier wears a long feather in his hat,
In his hat, hat, hat,
For the cavalier wears a long feather in his hat!"

Suppose you have lost all your treasure
(If you ever had any to lose),
You still have enough left for pleasure,
If you still have your legs and your shoes!

Come on, then, and trip us a measure,
  Round the merry May-pole in the dews;
Dance! The Sun dances up in the air,
  To the tune of "Away with the blues!"
      Sing, "Care hanged a cat,
      And Sorrow drowned a rat,
But the cavalier wears a long feather in his hat,
      In his hat, hat, hat,
For the cavalier wears a long feather in his hat;
      Hearts go pit-a-pat
      (Take that, that, and that).
Oh, the cavalier wears a long feather in his hat!"

BIRDS OF A FEATHER.

IMPORTUNE me no more,
  Close-fisted wife of mine,
Go in and shut the door,
  I go elsewhere to dine;
  For where the tapers shine
A score of good fellows be,
With whom till the night is late
  I purpose to have some wine
  (Scant in this house of thine),
And pledge old wives like thee,
Who hope to keep young husbands straight
  By holding the purse-strings tight.
  But, *pauca verba*, good-night!

—Have with you, boys! Birds of a feather
  Roost all night together;
    And whether
We gather in hall or heather,
  We bouse all night together!

GOOD-NIGHT.

I SAID to Fate, Let be,
Since I have done with thee,
Or heap upon my head
The ashes of the dead,
And huddle out of sight
The thing that once was me.
For when his head is white,
And he is poor and old,
'Tis time his grave was made;
Fetch mattock, then, and spade,
And let the bell be tolled.
And so, Sweet Fool, Good-night!

WHENCE AND WHITHER?

THIS is what he said in brief,
Sekasa, the Kaffir chief,
To the Frenchman, Arbrousset,
As beneath the palms they lay.

"I shepherded that time my flock
Twelve long years: then on a rock
I sat me down, thereon to mark
What would happen in the dark.
Questions many I asked, but none
Answered—could not answer one:
None who made the Stars, nor who
Taught them their dances in the blue.
Do the Waters, swift and bright,
As they flow from morn to night
Never weary of their race?
Whence and whither, to what place?
Where do they find rest,
In what arms, and on what Breast?
Whence and whither go the Clouds,
In wedding garments, and in shrouds?
Such imperishable crowds!
Whither away,
By night and day,
Like shadows over a magic glass,
Do they pass, and pass, and pass?
Weeping out themselves in rain,
They are falling now again.
What sends them,
And ends them,
And who when all is done, befriends them?
We have many a sharp diviner
(Though you French *savants* are finer),
But they do not fetch the rain,

Whence and Whither?

They have no means of making it,
Nor any chance of breaking it,
Nor do I see them, though I watch well,
Go for it, either to Heaven or Hell;
But somehow they seem to have the spell.
I cannot see the Wind,
Above, before, behind.
I know not whence it is,
Whether from bale, or bliss:
I feel what makes it come and go,
And rage, and worry, and roar,
For I live, you know, on the shore
Where the blasts of the desert blow.
But I shall never know
How the luscious corn doth grow.
Yesterday, yes, it was yesterday,
There was not a blade of grass in my field,
That is thick to-day as a warrior's shield;
For look to-day,
And look far away,
It is fresh and green,
And the sky over all is serene.
Who gave it this power to bring forth?
Who and what, save Earth,
Who folds us all in her broad arms' girth,
Our young, old Mother, the Earth?"

THE ARCHETYPAL MAN.

"*I hear the father of the ancient men.*"—BLAKE.

ON what historic page,
In what forgotten age,
Out of the world of night,
Rose this great Son of Light?
Did he run as the wild deer ran,
Down the slopes of Industan,
Rushing as tempests rush
Over the hills of the Hindu Kush,
Sheer into the Sacred River,
Whence none may deliver,
    On, still on,
    Till the last was gone,
Sunk in the Holy River?
Dropt from the peaks of Industan,
When the longest year is a span?
    Not from the East,
    Where life is a feast,
    Nor adrift from the North,
    Where Ice puts forth
From the gulf of the Boreal Sea—
    What time, or Place
    Produced the Race,
Forerunners of *you* and ME?

The Archetypal Man.

Dead, æons and æons ago,
Where wild winds blow,
Sifting and drifting Snow!
The caverns of France,
Where *damoiselles* dance,
On kitchen-middens remote,
On sunken piles,
In small Swiss isles,
Where shallops to-day still float:
Where we discover their barbèd hooks,
Which, unto scholars, are curious books,
Graven and carven of old,
With images manifold,
Writ with the primitive Pen
Of the Father of Ancient Men!
Shot headlong into the waves,
He rises in mountain caves,
Dark except for the light
Of the stalactite,
Still as the death lurking there
(Which nothing may spare),
In the sea-lion's maw,
And the bear's blunt paw,
Where the billows tumble in brine,
And many a vine
Trails hither and thither along,
Strange as the curlew's song!
There, where elk and deer,
Are scratched on the Elephant's tusk,

Where lingers the odor of musk
Like Summer all through the year!
What gods do they love—or fear?
The same whereunto we bow,
Idols that baffle us now;
Not wiser now than then,
Than Thou wert, O Father of Men!

FOUR GAZELES OF HAFIZ.

I.

O Wind! if thou should'st chance to pass the land,
The happy region, where my mistress is,
Bring me sweet scents from her ambrosial curls.

By her dear life it would fill my soul with bliss
An thou would'st fetch me a message from her heart.

If Heaven refuse this boon—why, then bring dust
To my two eyes from my beloved's house.

I pray that she may come—unhappy wretch!
When shall my weeping eyes behold her face?

I tremble like a reed, so strong my love
To see my fair one, stately as the pine.

Four Gazeles of Hafiz.

Albeit she love me not, I would not give
One hair of her dear head for all the world.

Though free from trouble, what does Hafiz gain,
Whose heart is but the slave of his Beloved?

II.

That beauteous idol with the stony heart,
And ornaments of silver in her ears,
She robs me of my reason and my rest.

Could I enfold her like the robe she wears,
Soon as I touched this robe, her inmost robe,
And clothed her with myself, my heart would rest.

If all my bones were mouldered into dust,
My soul could not forget its love for her.

Her neck and breast, her snow-white neck, her
breast,
They plunder me of my heart, my faith, and heart.

Hafiz, the only cure—the sovran cure,
Is in her full, sweet lips, her honeyed mouth.

III.

O balmy Wind! hast thou my mistress seen?
Thou must have stolen that musky scent from her;

Beware! thy fingers are too free by far,
For what hast thou to do with her bright curls?

O Rose! how can'st thou rival her red cheek?
Her cheek is smooth, but thine is rough with
thorns.

And how dar'st thou, Sweet Basil! sport thy
locks?
Her locks are glossy, thine are brown as dust.

And thou, Narcissus! wherefore gaze at her?
Her eyes are bright, but thine are dim with sleep.

O Cypress! when her stately form draws near,
Why wilt thou hope to be the garden's pride?

What would'st thou choose, O Wisdom! if to
choose
Were left thee still—in preference to Love?

Be patient, Hafiz! if thy love endure—
If may be thine, some day, to meet thy love.

IV.

If that fair maid of Shiraz would be mine,
I would Bokhara give, and Samarcand,
Just for the small, black mole upon her cheek:

Four Gazeles of Hafiz.

Go straightway, boy, and bring what wine remains;
We shall not find the banks of Rocnabad,
Nor the bowers of Mosellay, in Paradise.

Ah me, those wanton nymphs, those cunning girls,
For whose ripe charms Shiraz is up in arms—
They steal my peace of mind, my quiet heart.
They need not, dear ones, our imperfect love,
Fair faces need not perfume, paint, nor curls.

Discourse with me of minstrels and of wine,
Nor seek the secrets of Futurity;
No man can solve that riddle. Let it rest.
Love rules us all, but Beauty still rules Love;
Nor wonder, then, that Yussef's loveliness
Plucked off Zuleika's veil of modesty.

Hear sage advice, dear heart, for tender youths
Love old men's counsels better than their souls.
Thou speak'st ill of me, without offence;
May God forgive thee, thou hast spoken well;
But ah, do bitter words become thy mouth,
Those ruby lips, whence only sweetness falls?

Thou hast composed thy song, and strung thy pearls,
Now sing them sweetly, Hafiz, do thy best;
For heaven has sprinkled over all thy songs
The light and beauty of the Pleiades.

THE LADY OF THE EAST.

WHO art thou, Lady of the East,
  Whose day of eyes and night of hair
The daughter of a king, at least,
  Proclaim, so brightly, darkly fair?
Thy life is a perpetual feast,
  With but a single shadow there.

What is it, Lady? Some sweet thing
  Which once was thine, but now is fled?
Thy lute hath lost its golden string?
  Thy rose its freshest odor shed?
The bird thou lovest has taken wing,
  And to another sings instead?

What is it, Princess, that hath cast
  This sudden sadness on thy brow?
The shadow of what loving Past?
  The memory of what broken vow?
Girlhood hath gone from thee at last,
  And thou art perfect woman now.

I see thee as thou standest there
  With those mysterious eyes of thine,
And all that midnight length of hair,
  Like Dis's pall on Proserpine;

The Lady of the East.

I only know that thou art fair,
  I only wish that thou wert mine.

What Earth's first women were thou art,
  Glorious and gracious to behold,
With greater steadfastness of heart,
  Though cast in less heroic mould.
And yet with tears that sooner start,
  And smiles that were not known of old.

Thou hast no need to wear a crown,
  So royal in thyself art thou;
And whether Fortune smile, or frown,
  Thou hast the same unruffled brow;
Content if only men bow down
  And worship thee—as I do now.

I love thee, and will be to thee
  All that all men have been, and more;
Love me, and thou shalt be to me
  What never woman was before:
Be thou the shore, and I the sea,
  And let the great Sea kiss the shore.

ROMANCES FROM GUSTAVO BECQUER.

I.

I DARE behold thee asleep,
  Awake, I tremble and weep ;
So, life of my life, let me watch thee,
  While thou art asleep, asleep.

I press my hand on my heart,
  So wild are its beatings and deep,
Lest they trouble the peace of midnight,
  Where thou art asleep, asleep

I draw thy shutters close,
  And nightly my watch I keep,
Lest the dawn too early should wake thee,
  When thou art asleep, asleep.

II.

A tear was in her eye,
  But the tear was not shed ;
A word was on my lip,
  But the word was not said.

Why did we meet and part,
  So near that day, and dear?
Why was the word not said?
  And why not shed the tear?

III.

The vision of thine eyes
  Is ever in my mind,
Like the glory of the sun
  In the memory of the blind.

Wherever I may go,
  Lo, thou hast gone before;
I do not find thee there,
  Only thine eyes—no more.

They guide me to my room,
  They light me to my bed;
I feel them in my sleep
  Still watching o'er my head.

Marsh-fires that nightly lead
  The wanderer through the gloom;
So do thine eyes beguile—
  I know not to what tomb!

IV.

That she is proud, capricious, void of worth,
  I know, who long have suffered from her art;
Sooner shall water from a rock break forth
  Than feeling from her heart.

Woo her who will, her heart is still her own,
  Love seeks, but finds no answering fibre there;
Inanimate she is—a thing of stone—
  But oh, so fair, so fair!

V.

As in an open volume,
  I read your deep, deep eyes;
Why frame, then, shallow stories
  Which every glance belies?

That you a little loved me
  Be not ashamed to say;
If a man weeps (*I* am weeping),
  Be sure a woman may!

VI.

I sat on the edge of the bed,
  Where the lamp-light could not fall;
Silent, as though I were dead,
  With blank eyes fixed on the wall.

I sat on my bed alone,
  Till the long, dark night was done,
And in at the window shone
  The insolent light of the sun.

What terrible, nameless woe,
  What memories over me rolled,
I know not ; I only know
  I grew in that one night—old.

VII.

The dusky swallows will return,
  And, building as before,
Beneath your eaves their hanging nests,
  Will call their young once more.

But those that used to check their wings,
  As they flew along the shore,
To watch your beauty and my love—
  They will return no more.

The honeysuckles will return,
  And climb your garden wall,
And once more will their flowers unfold,
  When night begins to fall.

But those that earliest caught the dew,
  Beside your lattice-door,
And held it till the morn was come—
  They will return no more.

Once more the burning words of love
  Upon your ears may break,
And from its slumber long and deep
  Once more your heart may wake.

But speechless, kneeling at your feet,
  Like those who saints adore,
Though I may love you (as I shall)
  I shall return no more!

VIII.

Before thou diest I shall die,
  For in my heart I bear,
Bleeding to death, the cruel steel
  Thy hand hath planted there.

Before thou diest I shall die,
  But faithful still shall be,
For seated at the gate of death,
  My soul will wait for thee.

Day after day, year after year,
  Until thy life be past,
And at that portal thou shalt knock
  Where all must knock at last.

Then, when the earth is lying soft
  On thee—thy lips and eyes,
When plunged in death's baptismal stream
  Washed pure, thou shalt arise;

Out-of-Doors.

There, where the tumult of mankind
  Is heard and seen no more,
Gone, like the wind that raised the wave,
  The spent wave on the shore :

There, where to live is not to die,
  To love is not to fear—
We shall know all ; for we shall speak
  All that we spake not here !

OUT-OF-DOORS.

WRITING in-doors all my life,
As boy alone, as man with wife,
Prisoned close in city walls,
Where the sunlight seldom falls ;
With the coming on of age
I have slowly grown more sage,
In happier thoughts and higher lores,
Writing only out-of-doors.

Out-of-doors on a summer day,
Where the leaves are at their play,
Parleying with the fitful breeze,
Or the murmur of the seas ;
Seated here, in this old porch,
Youth returning waves his torch,
And my soul to song restores,
Singing and soaring out-of-doors.

UNCERTAIN SOUNDS.

THE wind in the leaves,
The rain on the eaves,
Or the low, continuous roar
Of the rolling waves on the distant shore :
Who shall declare
  What sounds they be ?
Whether lost in the air,
  Or found on the sea,
And whether they laugh, or sigh?
          Not I.
  I only know
That they come, and go,
And people the hollow sky.

MUSIC.

NEVER till now did I hear
In this close atmosphere
Of wind and whirling sand,
Or, hearing, understand,
The spells that in Music be;
    Nor by what secret laws
    The soul of man she draws,
As the orb of the Moon the Sea.

A Sailor Song.

Round after round
Of the ladder of sound
I follow her, higher, higher;
Like an arrow of light
Shot over the Night
By the Morning's bow of fire,
I cleave my way
To the spring of Day;
Where the airs are drifted along,
Heavy with odors of song.

A SAILOR SONG.

BOURBON and Braganza,
They say, are royal strains;
The blood of fifty sailors
Is running in my veins;
With a yo-heave-ho,
And a rumbelow!
Flowing, flowing,
Coming, going,
Not a waft in vain
To my little pinnace along the
Spanish main,
From dawn till day is done
To a sailor's son.

Implora Pacem.

The name that I bear
Means, they all declare,
Pennon, standard-bearer,
Stalwart armor-wearer,
Descendant of stout fellows,
Whom the Winter sun still mellows,
    With a yo-heave-ho,
    And a rombelow
To sailor sire and son.

IMPLORA PACEM.

WHY this ado art making?
  Wherefore and whence this sighing,
  This inward sobbing, crying?
Of whose woe art thou partaking?
  It will end at last with dying.
      Kyrie, eleyson.

Why art this low wail making?
  From whom art thou imploring?
  For what dear one's restoring?
Whose soul is life forsaking?
  O, what art thou adoring?
      Kyrie, eleyson.

No longer dirges making,
  No more of ceaseless sighing,

Wringing of hands and crying
(Asking, and no replying),
An end to thy heart-breaking!
All's over now, he's—dying!
Kyrie, eleyson.
CHRISTE, ELEYSON.

THE CAPTAIN'S SONG.

In my sluggish gait,
As it drags along of late,
Is the roll of the Captain on the deck;
Or the lurch of the sailor in the hold,
Courageous from of old,
In the storm and in the wreck;
In the rising, setting suns,
The thunder of the guns—
With a heave-and-a-ho
And a loud rumbelow;
In every sort of breeze,
On southern, northern seas,
Like a dancing leg,
At Old Wapping Stairs,
Where Meg, and Poll, and Peg
Are dancing unawares,
Like you, Bess, and me,
Near the margent of the sea;

To Julia.

At Oxford, or Cambridge, where ferrymen abound,
And merry men are found,
But sober, or tipsy,
Not the Scholar Gypsy,
Who forsook his learned books
For forests, streams, and nooks,
And was robbed, or was hanged, or was drowned,
Two hundred years ago—
With his heave and his ho,
And his mournful rombelow,
With not a soul to know,
Or to toll his passing knell,
His Ding-Dong-Bell.

TO JULIA.

SISTER of ours, child of the flowers,
With the dews of thy Maytime still wet,
Fair Julia, our dear Juliet,
Graced of the days and the hours,
Watched over by all the high Powers,
My best one, my own,
Queen on my throne,
The song I am singing is thine,
O, sister and daughter of mine.
Let thy soft eyes incline
To where in the darkness I pine,

Singing right out of my heart,
And not through the cold lips of art.
I kiss thee, my sweet,
Thy hands and thy feet,
Ah—all that is Thee!
Bestow of thy large love a little on me.

IN THE MEADOWS.

TRAMPING through the meadows,
In the summer day,
Under the blue arch of sky,
When the clouds go sailing by,
On their windy way;

Through the bending grasses,
Tall and lushy green,
All alive with tiny things,
Stirring feet and whirring wings,
Just an instant seen;

Down each fragrant hollow,
Up each little hill,
Leaping ditches, crossing brooks,
In the heart of shady nooks,
Fresh, and cool, and still;

In the Snow.

Past the spear-like rushes,
Swaying to and fro,
And along the river's bed,
Where grows the broad-leaved arrow-head—
I wonder where the bow?

Lost somewhere in the meadows,
Like what I meant to sing—
Who can tell what way it went?
Or lies it in my mind unbent,
A bow without a string?

IN THE SNOW.

NOT as in this winter's snow,
Where, while lost therein, I see
No one out of doors but me;
No one in the buried street,
Nor in the cold blast of the sleet;
But five-and-twenty years ago,
When beneath a hostile star,
The whole land was wrapt in war
(Naught to hope, but much to fear),
When these long embankments here
Were projected, not in white
But in great earth-works of red clay,
Low in the morning, high at night,

I tramp through the meadows, sad and slow,
Where the distant bugles seem to blow
Back to that burning August day!

HOW AND WHY.

If one could understand
The things that are close at hand,
The How and the Why,
He never need die.
The flowers which bloom,
With their hidden perfume,
Where the spider weaves in its fairy loom;
The rivulet which sings
Of the far-off springs;
The leaf on the tree,
Dancing in glee
To an inward melody;
Trees, spiders, flowers declare
Secrets of earth and air,
And all make reply:
"O man, you need not die."
But there cometh—from where?
This voice of despair.
"The order of Nature
Doth this way tend;
Whatever was begun
Will surely have an end."

MORS ET VITA.

"UNDER the roots of the roses,
Down in the dark, rich mould,
The dust of my dear one reposes
Like a spark which night incloses
When the ashes of day are cold."

"Under the awful wings
Which brood over land and sea,
And whose shadows nor lift nor flee—
This is the order of things,
And hath been from of old;
First production,
And last destruction;
So the pendulum swings,
While cradles are rocked and bells are tolled."

"*Not* under the roots of the roses,
But under the luminous wings
Of the King of kings
The soul of my love reposes,
With the light of morn in her eyes,
Where the Vision of Life discloses
Life that sleeps not nor dies."

"Under or over the skies
What is it that never dies?

Spirit—if such there be—
  Whom no one hath seen nor heard,
We do not acknowledge thee ;
  For, spoken or written word,
Thou art but a dream, a breath ;
Certain is nothing but Death ! "

THOUGHT.

ACROSS the tense chords
  Thought runs before words,
Brighter than dew,
  And keener than swords.
Whence it cometh,
  And whither it goes,
All may conjecture,
  But no man knows.
  It ebbs and flows
  In the dance of the leaves,
  The set of summer eaves,
The scent of the violets, the odor of the rose.

THE SINGER.

THE only good method
  Of head or of heart,
Is the one which produces
  The perfectest art.

A Fantasy.

The voice of the lark,
  As it rings on high,
Was begot in the dark
And flung like a spark
  Out into the sky,
With the clouds below,
Like mountains of snow
  And day near by.
  So the lark sings,
  With light on his wings,
And so, when I can, do I.

A FANTASY.

OR worsted, or bettered,
  In the combat of wit,
By lettered, or unlettered,
  I cheerfully submit ;
For, bumpkin or cit,
  You must not think me cruel,
  If winning this duel,
I parry with my poniard your misdirected wit.
  For the weapon that I wear
  Is *le sabre de mon père*,
  Who fell at Quatre-Bras,
  And was mangled by the paw
  Of the gory British lion,
In sight of Waterloo, a happy field to die on,

In the rainy afternoon
Of that awful day in June,
To the foolish old tune—
I can hear it still afar—
Of *Malbrook s'en va-t-en guerre,*
With its sonorous refrain,
That was never heard in vain,
Of "*Mironton, Mironton, Mirontaine.*"

VOX CLAMANTIS.

SHOUTED a voice to me,
  In the silence of a dream
  From the sedgy banks of a stream,
In the bed of a sunken sea—
    Time lost in Eternity,
    As I am lost in thee,
    O, why not thou in me,
        Perdita?

Perdita, dear one, flown,
Leaving me here alone,
What else can I do but be
Rivulet, brooklet to thee,
Best of the best in me,
As I am the worst of thee,
Queen of my soul's high throne,
My darling, my love, my own,
        PERDITA!

CHILDREN'S SONGS.

I.

"WHERE is the little lark's nest,
  My father showed to me?
And where are the pretty lark's eggs?"
  Said Master Lori Lee.
At last he found the lark's nest,
  But eggs were none to see.

"Why are you looking down there?"
  Sang two young larks near by:
"We've broken the shell that held us,
  And found a nest on high."
And the happy birds went singing
  Far up the summer sky!

II.

"There's a little mill a-going,
    I hear its whirr again."
"No; 'tis but the house-fly
    Buzzing in the pane."

"Tis not a fly, but a fairy,
    Such as dance in magic rings;
A wee, elfish miller,
    With a wheel beneath his wings!

And his grist is the sunshine
  Which through the window there
Into golden meal is powdered,
  That dances in the air."

III.

"I hope you'll not accuse me,
  But excuse me,"
Said the simple Bee to the royal red Rose,
"If I take a pot of honey,
  And don't put down the money,
For, alas, I haven't any, as all the world knows.

"Mister Bee, don't worry,
  Nor be sorry,"
Said the queenly Rose to the poor, yeoman Bee :
"You've paid me for my honey
  Much better than with money
In the sweet songs of Summer you sing and sing
  to me!"

IV.

Why did the snow keep falling?
  What did the March winds say?
And why, when Earth was a-flowering,
Was April showering, showering?
  I know, I know to-day.

The apple blossoms have told me,
  And the twinkling dew on the spray,
They wanted to change their places,
And, putting on shining faces,
  To be the beautiful May.

V.

"Give me a month," said the Summer,
  Demanding of Nature a boon,
"That shall make surly Winter forgotten,
  And be with all sweet things in tune.

The skies must be blue, the Sun golden,
  Love must light the white lamp of the Moon."
The great Mother smiled, and kissed her,
  And the smile and the kiss were—June!

VI.

When my ships come home from sea,
O how happy I shall be!
And my darling children, too,
Lorimer, and Bess, and Sue;
They shall share, and share with me,
When my ships come home from sea.

Lori shall have a silver hoop,
  And a whistle of yellow gold;

And, every marble an agate,
  More marbles than he can hold,
Never a boy so glad as he,
When my ships come home from sea.

And what shall Bessie have?
  A comb of mother-of-pearl;
A diamond rose to light up her hair,
And never queen alive shall wear
  Such robes as my sweet girl!
Many's the kiss she'll give to me,
When my ships come back from sea.

Sarah shall have a Paris doll,
  That will wink with a knowing air;
And dishes of old, pink China,
  And such a love of a chair!
O how happy all will be
When my ships come back from sea.

When will my ships come back?
  As near as I can remember,
When the rose of June shall be blowing
  In the cold winds of December;
  Or when the snow of December
Drifts on the buds of June,
  At twelve o'clock at midday,
Under the light of the moon.
Be sure, if sleeping, to waken me,
For then my Ships will have come from Sea!

FATHER AND CHILD.

WE sat and talked together,
  My little boy and I;
It was changeful April weather,
  And rain was in the sky.
A wintry wind was blowing,
  The sun refused to shine;
This set his tongue a-going,
  As if the fault were mine.

"You are the crossest father
  (And mother says so, too),
I ever had. I'd rather
  Have none at all than you.
You said I might go walking,
  And don't do what you say;
You try to stop my talking,
  You will not let me play.

If all the fathers living
  Were children, you would see
What things they would be giving
  To little boys like me.
You'd get me all I needed,
  A pair of gloves and cane,
(There's Sidney's father, he did,)
  Besides a watch and chain.

Father and Child.

It always makes me sorry
  Whenever I am told
That I am only Lori,
  And only eight years old;
That I am not a hundred,
  A great, big man like you:
And I have often wondered
  What I would be and do.

No father to compel me
  To do, or leave undone,
No mother then to tell me
  I was a naughty son.
I want to grow old faster,
  I hurry all I can;
I'll be my own free master
  When I become a man!"

Forgetting he had teased me,
  I smiled at what he said,
For something in it pleased me,
  Although I shook my head.
I said: "You are mistaken,
  My child, in thinking so."
With confidence unshaken
  He stoutly answered, "No."

"My boy, I can remember
  When I was young, I say;

For though in Life's December,
  My heart is true to May.
Before I was a father
  I was a child, you see.
If you were me, you'd rather
  Be you, my dear, than me.

No father's hand caressed me,
  I knew no father's love;
If when he died he blessed me
  Is only known above.
Somewhere in ocean, may be—
  I know not—he may rest,
For I was but a baby
  Upon my mother's breast.

My childhood was not pleasant,
  For, unlike you, my boy,
I never had a present,
  And never bought a toy.
Yet, hard as this seems, Lori,
  I felt so little pain,
I would be glad, not sorry,
  To be that child again.

When I am worn and weary,
  And I am both to-day,
For everything looks dreary,
  And mother is away;

And strange, new troubles gather,
  And my poor head is wild—
I am sick of playing Father,
  I want to be the Child!"

OUR FATHERS.

HERE where our fathers worshipped in the Past,
And where their children worship now, we come,
With reverent spirit, as befits the place,
The house they builded for their heavenly needs,
On this green hill, two hundred years ago.
Averse from ceremonious forms and rites,
They left their dear, ancestral homes, the graves
Wherein the ashes of their dead reposed.
They crossed a thousand stormy leagues of sea,
Bearing the best of England in their breasts,
And planted the New World in the wilderness.
Masterful men, but narrow, quick to do
The work that seemed appointed to their hands;
Content with little pleasures, or with none;
Not troubled with unprofitable thoughts;
Of one thing sure—that God would judge them all.
Their sturdy virtues were the corner-stone
Whereon were set the pillars of the State.
Their lives were hard. They tilled the stubborn
  soil,

Our Fathers.

Beset with peril from their savage foes,
Or ploughed the windy furrows of the deep,
Under the Pole Star or the Southern Cross,
Adventurous, resolute, their creed summed up
In the right to worship God in their own way,
And not as priests ordain. They had it here.
Here, where their marriage-vows were interchanged,
Their children were baptized, and where at last,
When the long pilgrimage of life was done,
The mourners bore their bodies. Graves were dug
On the green hillside, where their fathers slept,
And they were buried there with many tears,
With homely headstones, carved with cherubs' wings,
And under these the years of birth and death,
And pious texts of Scripture, which declared
That, dying in the Lord, the dead were blessed ;
For there remains a rest for them, a house
Not built with hands, eternal in the heavens.
Such hope, such certainty, our fathers had ;
Such hope, such certainty, such rest be ours.

THOUGHTS FOR THANKSGIVING.

If gracious smiles are met with smiles,
  And who would meet them otherwise?
And tender words persuade the heart,
Till tears, kept back, unbidden start
  In dry and unfamiliar eyes:

If acts of courtesy like these,
  The common coin of every day,
Pass current everywhere, and make
So many richer for their sake,
  For none can be too poor to pay:

What shall be, can be, said for those
  Who greater gifts their whole lives long
Receive without acknowledgment,
Receive, perhaps, with discontent,
  Without a thankful word, or song?

Time was they were not, now they are;
  A Power by them unseen, unknown,
Produced them, not to die like flowers,
Poor pensioners of summer hours,
  For they remain, though years are flown.

Thoughts for Thanksgiving.

From nothingness to conscious Life,
  That feels itself if nought beside,
And straightway all it sees demands,
Perpetually puts forth its hands
  To take, and will not be denied ;

That such a creature, selfish, frail,
  One-half whose days are passed in sleep,
Watched over by maternal eyes,
Which, when its small breath comes in sighs,
  Tremble, and ready are to weep :

That childhood should in manhood end
  Is strange as childhood just begun.
Why did he live ? He might have died.
What made Death's arrows glance aside ?
  The Power of Life and Death in one.

This he perceives not, or forgets,
  For now because he lived he lives ;
He has his raiment, and his food,
Accepts what comes, and finds it good,
  And never thinks of Him who gives.

Something he sought he may have missed,
  Or in his heart, or in his brain ;
Fame, power, wealth, love. If so, what then ?
Blot all these from the lives of men,
  Still Man, and Life, and Earth remain.

Thoughts for Thanksgiving.

The sun still rises as of gold ;
  The stars and planets shine on high ;
The great Sea laughs ; clouds come and go ;
Rains fall ; birds sing ; the sweet flowers blow ;
  And fragrant is the west wind's sigh.

O Earth, thou art a goodly world !
  And who deny, if such there be,
The Power that placed them here, should own,
Thou Symbol of that Power Unknown,
  Their endless gratitude to thee !

They breathe the airs that stir thy trees ;
  Thy sunshine is their constant light ;
Without thy harvests they would die,
Their sustenance and sole supply ;
  They lie, and slumber in thy Night.

But say thou art no more, O Earth !
  Than we behold from day to day,
An Inn, we travellers, thou at least
Hast spread us many a bounteous feast
  And comforted upon the way !

We thank thee, and through thee the Host,
  Who has provided of His best,
And housed us so we hate to go ;
For we can never hope to know
  More watchful care, more perfect rest.

DECORATION DAY.

I WALKED the streets at midnight,
  But my thoughts were far away ;
For my leaf of life now withered
  Was green again with May.

The snows of twenty winters
  Had vanished from my brow,
And I,—ah me,—looked forward,
  As I look backward now.

Why should I not look forward ?
  I knew my soul was strong ;
I knew there was within me
  The might there is in Song.

My heart was light and friendly,
  I loved my fellow-men,
And I loved—how much—my comrades,
  For I had comrades then.

Where are those dear old fellows ?
  Ah, whither have they flown ?
I asked myself at midnight,
  As I walked the streets alone.

Decoration Day.

There was Fitz, the Irish singer,
  And Fred, the tender heart,
And Harry, who lived for Woman,
  And Tom, who lived for Art.

Poor Fitz's song is over,
  And the heart of Fred is still;
One went down at Yorktown,
  The other at Malvern Hill.

Wrapt in the blue they fought in,
  They buried them where they lay;
And elsewhere Tom and Harry,
  Who wore, poor lads, the gray.

As I walked the streets at midnight,
  And remembered the awful years
That snatched my comrades from me,
  My eyes were filled with tears.

I thought of bloody battles,
  Where thousands such as they
Had met and killed each other
  For wearing the blue and the gray.

Of happy homes that were darkened,
  Of hearths that were desolate,
Of tender hearts that were broken,
  Of love that was turned to hate.

Decoration Day.

I pitied the wretched living,
  I think I did the dead ;
I know I sighed for Harry,
  And dropped a tear for Fred.

" Poor boys ! " I said. But pondering
  What was, and might have been
(What I am in the sere leaf,
  And they were in the green).

I pitied my dead no longer ;
  I did not dare to. No.
They went when they were summoned,
  Before, they could not go.

When we know what Life and Death are,
  We shall then know which is best ;
Meanwhile we live and labor :
  Their labor done, they rest.

The earth lies heavy on them,
  But they do not complain ;
They do not miss the sunshine,
  They do not feel the rain.

If they are ever conscious,
  In that long sleep of theirs,
It is when, past the winter,
  We feel the first spring airs.

Hair of Washington.

When the birds from tropic countries
  Come back again to ours,
And where of late were snow-drifts,
  The grass is thick with flowers ;

Such flowers as will to-morrow
  Be scattered where they lie,
The blue and gray together,
  Beneath the same sweet sky.

No stain upon their manhood,
  No memory of the Past,
Except the common valor
  That made us One at last.

HAIR OF WASHINGTON.

THE relics of the great
  Who by the sword or pen
Create or save the State
  Should precious be to men ;
Preserved and reverenced long
  For every deed they wrought
That lessened human wrong,
  And broadened human thought.

Sacred to me the shred
  Of thin, white hair I hold,

To Mary Bradley.

Cut from a great man's head
  When he in death was cold
Of English blood, he rose
  Superior to his race,
For, when he might, he chose
  Nor rich reward, nor place.

Steadfast for all the sword
  Of Sidney, Milton's pen,
Established, or restored,
  More potent now than then.
Of all my relics chief,
  Preserve his just renown,
Outlast the latest leaf
  Of Cæsar's laurel crown.

TO MARY BRADLEY.

I SHALL behold, I hope I shall behold
Before the rainfall of to-morrow night,
A woman loved of old, who is not old,
To whom before I was my heart was plight.
My name with hers in Fate's great book enrolled,
Shines, as it ought to, in supernal light,
Twins, slumbering, smiling, on the arm of might,
The mystery of our being still untold.

To William James Linton.

I know this woman—no one half so well—
Your love as well as mine, diviner Powers!
Whose currents, shifting always, seldom vary;
For she was born beneath a gracious spell,
Somewhere and somehow in the countless hours
Before I Richard was, or she was Mary!

TO WILLIAM JAMES LINTON.

MY dear friend, Linton, if your purpose hold,
And adverse fates at last propitious be,
You must be plunging through the starless sea
Between your world and ours, which is more old;
Weltering, I fear, where stormy waves are rolled,
And Arctic icebergs Spring has now set free,
Out of the darkness slowly drift a-lee,
Freighted, like life, with death's eternal cold.
But why should this foreboding heart of mine
Create disasters for you? Why deplore
What the long leagues of tempest-battered shore
May never swallow in their yeasty brine?
What said Sir Humphrey, tiller-ropes in hand?
"Heaven is as near by water as by land."

AT A DINNER OF ARTISTS.

SITTING beside you in these halls to-night,
Begirt with kindly faces known so long,
My heart is heavy though my words are light,
So strangely sad and sweet are art and song.
Twin sisters, they, at once both bright and dark,
Clinging to coming hours and days gone by,
When hope was jubilant as a morning lark,
And memory silent as the evening sky.
Where are the dear companions, yours and mine,
Whom for one little hour these walls restore,
Courteous and gracious, of a noble line,
And happy times that will return no more?
Farewell and hail! We come and we depart:
I, with my song (ah me!), you, with your art.

AT WASHINGTON.

WHAT constitutes a State? Not arms, nor arts,
Stout sinews, nor the will that makes them strong;
It is upbuilded in heroic hearts,
Self-circling from a more than spheral song.
Before it, like light clouds, the years disperse,
Parting to-day above this stately dome,

Within whose pillared halls the hours rehearse
More tragic issues than dispeopled Rome.
Behold yon marble shaft that cleaves the skies,
Far-seen beyond the circuit of the hills ;
And gathered here a host with reverent eyes,
Whose depths, unsunned, the light of freedom fills,
And *he* whom these have chosen—if not great,
Great through their choice, who were, and are, the
State.

MORITURUM SALUTAMUS.

It is most fitting he should pass away,
As he is passing now without a word,
This man of many battles, whom Dismay
Dismayed not, whose stout heart was seldom
stirred.
Master of his emotions—not too keen,
Of simple, primitive tastes, his wants were few ;
Believer only in things known and seen,
Stubborn and blunt, begotten to subdue.
Not his the blood in Sidney's veins which ran,
Nor his who fell at Roncesvalles of old ;
But there is something in this silent man,
Something heroic in his rugged mould.
Of this our Soldier dying Time will be
A kinder, sterner, juster judge than we.

ON NEARING THE SECOND CATARACT.

WHEN I was young—ah, distant when—
And just began to hold my pen,
My head obeyed my tardy hand,
Submissive to its least command;
But now that I have older grown,
And more of other authors known,
I understand how Milton wrote
With younger fingers than his own
The Fall of Man—the tragic note
That struggled through Samson's rugged lines,
Blind, like himself, among the Philistines.

THE CROSSING OF THE WAYS.

(*John Eliot Bowen.*)

DID I see it, or does it seem,
In some world of classic dream?
Who knows this is more wise than I,
It was so distant, is so nigh.
Where ruined tombs and temples stand,
In a many-peopled land,

The Crossing of the Ways.

Where are coming, going ways,
Where many haste, but no one stays,
Toward which a man with eager gaze
Urges forward, fair and fleet,
With gold sandals on his feet :
I dream of him by night and day,
At once so serious and gay,
Leaves of November, buds of May,
Wreathed with myrtle, crowned with bay ;
Two natures in him, gentle, bold,
Affections young, but judgment old,
Over him their light and shadow plays,
As he nears the crossing of the ways.
But who are These, that fast, or slow,
Seem now to come, and now to go ?
One stealing silently along,
The other marching with bursts of song ;
One clad in a waving, yellow robe,
Such as Summer all over the globe
Wears at the earliest flush of June,
When the hearts of all things are in tune.
But the other, that ominous other,
Twinned of the same great Mother,
Why differs he so from his brother ?
Visions and apparitions fly,
Here before them, and there behind,
Those to loosen, and these to bind,
As the hours delay, and the days go by.
Each bravely holds aloft his torch,

That lights the tombs, and a temple-porch.
But now that they reach the altar,
And stand by the sacred fires,
The bride and the groom both falter,
For the flame of one torch expires.
What more? In my dream remains
The end of my friend—not my pains.
He is gone; he will not return;
Nothing left us here but—an Urn.

AT CONCORD.

BLOWN round the stormy Capes,
And in along the Sound,
Haunted by shadows, or shapes,
Out of the night profound
The Muse of the New World came
With wings and sandals of fire,
Flashed hither like sunset flame,
Or the lightning speed of desire,
Rushing along on a wind of song
From the weary waste of the sea,
To me, who have worshipped her long—
O why hath she come to me?
Because the Angel of Fate,
Whose name is also Death,
Passing from east to west,

At Concord.

Its secret errand not guessed,
In impious pride elate,
Laid violent hands on the great,
And plucked from his hoary head
The crowns of the world whose breath
Is heavy with eastern blooms,
That swoon with their own perfumes,
And those that rise under western skies,
Out of the Isles of the Blest,
With promise of endless rest,
Such as fills the sacred breast
Of this great, good man who is dead.

With heads bent down, and slow,
Where to-day do ye go,
People of Concord, and why
Are those tears unshed in the eye
Of man, and woman, and child,
That follow like souls exiled ?
But who and what do they follow
To that grave in Sleepy Hollow,
Fresh dug in the warm, rich ground,
Where flowers will soon abound,
Roses, violets—all
That the Mother's hands let fall,
Scattering dew on the sod
Where his feet so often have trod,
Before the clouds on his soul
Began to gather, and roll,

And the iron bell to toll?
What is that clamor of thine,
O Bell! that art sounding afar,
Like a cry flung down from a star—
Hearken—"*Seventy-nine!*"
A great many years to live
Where all is so fugitive.
He came of a clerical stock
For eight long generations,
Which stood as firm as a rock
In the anger of battling nations.
His grandsire marched with his flock
On that famous April morn
When the Old World died, and the New was born—
There, over yon rustic bridge,
Posted before the western ridge
On the bank of the river, full-fledged with pines,
Where aslant on their needles the morning shines,
And where, by a night's swift march, there came,
Smoke their vanguard, their rearguard Flame—
Veterans of Wolfe, and Marlborough,
Who fought their way through the Countries Low,
At Blenheim, Ramillies, Malplaquet,
Who looked on warfare as manly play—
With banners ablaze, like summer noons,
Fifers playing the merriest tunes,
Tired foot-soldiers, mounted dragoons,
Eight hundred strong, till the stern word *Halt*

Arrests them on the bridge at fault,
For they dare not retreat, and dare not assault.
"Men of Concord," the preacher cried,
Bible in hand, and son by his side,
"Stand." They stood. "They shall not advance."
The light of his eye was a brandished lance.
"Make ready, *Present*." Then, at the word,
"It is not I who speak, but the Lord—
FIRE!" The varlets were soon on the run,
Scouring the road to Lexington,
Their proud crests sunken, their banners furled—
Scared by the shot heard round the world!
That a race like this should baffle their king,
Stout fighters all, was a foregone thing.
A hundred and forty years before
They had settled the place, which then was a wild,
Begirt with wigwams, at whose door,
Bow in hand, and arrow thereon,
(Like the disk and light of the sun),
Stood the savage, and grimly smiled
At the pale-faced strangers, who were not afraid,
For they straightway builded a strong stockade,
That shut their foes out, and shut in
Their wives and daughters, famine-thin,
Shaking with agues, with fevers down,
But stubbornly bent to found the town.
And they did. For when such races meet,
Not strongest hands, nor swiftest feet,

Nor all the useless blood they shed,
Determines which shall lose or win,
For victory, when they begin,
Selects the white race—not the red.
It conquers here, nor all by blows,
But half by the subtle craft of its foes :
It tracks them as they track the bear,
Under their feet a constant snare,
And with a speed that never fails
Pursues them on their viewless trails ;
Comes without warning, far off is nigh,
Gone in the twinkling of an eye—
What can the red men do but die ?
Children of Nature, which no more
Shelters and saves them, they transfer
To the wits they sharpen all the lore
That they contrived to wrest from her :
Motions of spring under winter snow,
What happens when certain birds fly low,
Where squirrels conceal their nests, and bees
Deposit their honey in hollow trees ;
Promise of winds, when wind is none,
As this or that way rushes bend ;
Presage of clouds, and moon, and sun,
And what the Northern Lights portend.
Secrets of the Solar Year
Became the birthright of our seer,
With what the fearless scholar finds
In cosmic myths, which primitive minds

Writ large, but with an earlier pen
Than chronicled the deeds of men ;
Scriptures of races, old and new,
The Hebrew prophet, the rapt Hindu ;
And what with Hesiod, Homer began—
Mutable gods, with passions of man ;
The cunning that shaped the Doric frieze,
The grace and greatness of Pericles,
Socratic question, Platonic dream,
What hallowed the grove of Academe,
With what the Christian Fathers said,
(Greatest of dead, which are not dead),
Saints Chrysostom and Augustine,
And the Roman of imperious line—
The Marcus we call Antonine ;
All to this wise man was clear,
All to this great man was dear :
Was—but is not ; for to-day
He has gone upon his way,
As the Masters went before,
And will be with us no more.

He has earned the right to rest,
And we should be comforted ;
For the simple life he led,
And the love that he professed
For all wisdom—are not dead.
Spirits such as his remain
In the noble things they wrought,

Whereof the whole to men belong ;
His, in grave and gracious thought,
And in the high poetic strain
That is the burden of his Song.

AT ROSLYN.

(*November* 3, 1884.)

WHEN poets touch the heart, they touch
  To finer issues than the brain
  Conceives of either joy or pain ;
And their sweet influence is such
  As comes to buds with vernal rain.

Sculpture may satisfy the eye
  With lines of grandeur or of grace ;
  Painting restore the hour, the place,
When tranced with wood, or wave, or sky,
  We stood with Nature face to face.

And Music—all that spells of sound,
  Enamoured of melodious speech,
  Rejoice in, calling, answering each,
Music may bring ; but more profound
  Than these the arts that poets teach.

At Roslyn.

Their Art is Nature. They divine
  Her secrets, and to man disclose ;
  They taught, or teach, him all he knows,
First, last, of the prophetic line,
  And what he is, and where he goes.

Of many men and many things
  Forgetful, priests that shape his creed,
  Stout men-at-arms that make him bleed,
He still remembers him who sings,
  Who was, and is, his friend indeed.

Green was the laurel Cæsar wore,
  But Virgil's wreath is greener now
  Than Cæsar's ; that imperial brow
Is balder than it was before,
  Powerless ; but, Horace, not so thou.

A Queen and player both drew breath
  In good old England's golden prime :
  To-day the sovereign of that time
Is Shakespeare, not Elizabeth,
  Not Tudor, but his powerful rhyme.

What homage shall we offer these,
  Our Masters, and their deathless song ?
  Pay them the honors that belong
To founders of great dynasties
  The strong hands that destroy the strong ;

At Roslyn.

Build monuments to them beside
  Earth's mighty ones, theirs mightiest;
  Visit the spots that knew them best,
The houses where they lived and died,
  The graves wherein their ashes rest.

Master! The monument we raise
  Is other than these piles of stone.
  Builded by Nature's hands alone,
Before thee all thy length of days,
  'Tis near thee now that thou art gone.

Poet of Nature! Thou to her
  Wast dearest of this Western race;
  And she whom thou wast first to trace,
Discoverer and worshipper—
  She folded thee in her embrace!

A child, she led thee hand in hand,
  To watch the grassy rivulet flow,
  Where still the yellow violets grow,
And still the tall old forests stand,
  Though that was ninety years ago.

What monument so fit as these,
  Which never from their poet's heart
  Were absent—in the noisy mart,
Or in strange lands beyond the seas,
  Where still he walked with them apart?

Bring these! O bring the forest trees
From Cummington to Roslyn now!
He would be glad to know they bow
Above him in the summer breeze,
And have their shadows on his brow.

Memorial in Cathedral vast
He needeth none, nor requiem, save
The music of the wind and wave;
Least such a song as this I cast
Like a poor wild flower on his grave.

THE JUDGMENT OF SOLOMON.

ONCE on a time, when he was growing old,
Albeit there was no sign of age in him,
Except his snowy beard, King Solomon
Sat deeply meditating on his throne,
His magic throne, which bore him where he would,
Winged like a planet. On a mountain-peak,
Which overlooked the long Iranian plain,
And many-citied kingdoms of the Ind,
It stood, like morn re-risen in the east,
Seen by the people over whom it shone,
And seen of every creature of the earth,
Which gathered from all quarters of the earth,
Commanded thither by the powerful word

Of their imperious master, Solomon,
Whom the four angels of the land and sea
Had given dominion over them and theirs,
That they should honor him and do his will,
And who, moreover, understood their speech,
And could converse with them, so wise was he.
Surrounded there by these that summer day
He sat, and over him the birds of heaven
Hung motionless, a living canopy
That shut out the fierce sunlight; also came
And ministered to him the winds of heaven,
They, or the angels who ruled over them,
Diverse in kind, but strangely beautiful,
As when with their innumerable wings
He first beheld them in Jerusalem.
The populous kingdoms of the earth and air,
Below, above, about him, troubled him,
Troubled him because he understood their speech,
Their habits, passions, everything they were,
What life was to them, and how short it was,
And, whether long or short, how certain death.
The solemn thought of their mortality,
And, it may be, his own, which all that day
Was present with him, an unwelcome guest,
The more unwelcome as he grew more old,
Darkened the loving heart of Solomon,
Darkened his soul, till, lifting up his eyes,
He saw a mist which slowly shaped itself,
Or seemed to shape, into an odorous cloud,

Which rose before him, and from out the cloud
There reached a hand that held a crystal cup,
Filled with strange water, clearer than the cup;
And sweeter than all music spake a voice,
Saying: "The Maker of the Universe—
His Name and Power be honored, glorified,
Hath sent me with this cup, wherein thou seest
The waters of youth and everlasting life.
Choose freely whether thou wilt or wilt not drink,
This draught of youth and everlasting life.
Think, wilt thou be immortal through all time,
Or live and die like other men? I wait."
Deep silence brooded over all the Place
When the Voice ceased, and Solomon communed
Within himself upon the thing he heard.
Firm as a pillar stood the odorous cloud,
And the white hand reached out the diamond cup,
"Surely," he thought, "the gold of life is good
To spend in the great market of the world;
Fruitful the soil of life, wherein to plant
The stately palms of power, the flowers of love;
But joyless is the dark repose of death."
Thus he, within the silence of his thoughts
Debating life and death. "Before I drink
I will take other counsel than mine own;
For though men call me wise, I know myself
Foolish at times—I think more foolish now
That age hath come on me." He summoned then
All spirits which were subject to his charge,

The angels of the winds and of the seas,
The birds of heaven, the creatures of the earth,
The souls of wise men dead before he lived,
And speaking to them in their several tongues,
Demanded they should tell him, if they knew,
Whether, indeed, it would be wise in him
To drain the cup of everlasting life,
Or let it go, and die like other men.
Then, like the voices of a thousand streams
Which are one voice, the countless multitude
Straightway entreated him to drain the cup,
Seeing that the welfare of the world was laid
Upon his wisdom, as upon the hills,
That hold up the high heavens. And, furthermore,
The happiness of all things was sustained
By the perfected circle of his life,
Set like a jewel in a golden ring,
The precious jewel in his signet-ring,
Which was the Incommunicable Name.
He hearkened to their voices, hearkening more
To the unspoken longing in his heart,
Of which they were the answer ; then, resolved,
Stretched forth his hand and took the shining cup,
Whereat the hand that gave it into his,
Tempting, withdrew into the pillared cloud.
Wondrous the lights within the water were,
Which water was no longer, but a wine
The like whereof no mortal ever saw,

Not pressed from earthly clusters such as grew
In his walled garden of Jerusalem—
Vintage of heaven, its rare aroma stole,
Like the remembered music of a dream,
Through all his senses, yearning with delight.
And, lo! from out its living depths a flame
Flashed suddenly up, and flushed his royal face,
Prophetic promise of returning Youth.
He would have drank, but something stayed his hand,
Some dark foreboding that he had not done
All that a wise man should to know the truth.
Perhaps he had misheard the unknown voice
That spake from out the cloud—the words were strange;
Perhaps his wily servants flattered him,
Puffed up with self-importance. He would see.
"O ye," he cried, "who minister to me,
Spirits, and men, and creatures of the earth,
Tell me if there be any absent now,
Many, or one, for I commanded all
To meet me here at noon." And they replied,
Bowing before the might of Solomon,
"Master, the only one who is not here
Is that most loving of all living things,
Whom all things love, the wild dove Boutimar."
The Lord of Learning sent a golden bird,
A marvellous gift from Sheba's beauteous Queen,
To find and fetch the wild dove Boutimar

From where her nest was builded on the roof
Of the great Temple of Jerusalem.
The glory of the reign of Solomon.
"O dove," he said, while she was still afar,
"Wild dove that dwellest in the clefts of rocks,
Or in the hiding-places of the wood,
Singing all day, 'The fashion of this world
Passes away like stubble in the fire,
But God remains eternal in the heavens.'
Hither, my dove, and let me see thy face,
Hither, and let me hear thy voice once more."
Then when the wild dove Boutimar was come,
Smoothing her feathers with a tender hand,
He bade her tell him whether it were best
That he, her lord and master, Solomon,
Should drink the waters of immortal youth.
Whereunto Boutimar, the Bird of Love,
Whose wisdom was proportioned to her love:
"How should a simple creature of the sky,
Tenant of lonely places far from men,
In rocky clefts, or woods, or temple roofs,
Answer the Master of Intelligence?
Yet if it must be that I counsel thee,
Instruct me whether this bright Cup of Life
Be for thee only, or for all mankind."
And he: "It hath been sent to me alone.
There is not in the cup another drop,
Nay, not so much as the least bead of dew
Left at high noontide in the lily's leaves."

" Prophet of God ! " the wild dove answered then,
" O, how couldst thou desire to live alone,
Then, when thy trusty friends and counsellors,
Thy wives, thy children, all who love thee, all
Whom thou dost love, are numbered with the
dead ?
For these must surely drink the cup of death,
Though thou to-day shouldst drink the cup of life.
Who could endure eternal youth, O King,
When the world's face was wrinkled with old age,
And Death's black fingers, reaching everywhere,
Had closed the pale eye of the latest star ?
When all thou lovest shall have passed away
Like smoke of incense in that holy House
Which thou hast builded in Jerusalem ;
When, poor, dead dust, the heart that beat to thine
Shall have been scattered by the winds of heaven ;
When eyes which were the loadstars of thy fate
Have left not even the memory of their light;
When voices which were music in thine ears
Are mute forever; when thy life shall be
The sole oasis in the waste of death,
Eternal recognition of the dead,
Wilt thou then care to live, O Solomon ?
Or, rather, wilt thou die like the wild dove
Who perishes when its truant mate comes not ? "
For answer Solomon restored the cup
To the white hand, that disappeared again
Deep in the dense concealment of the cloud,

Which in a moment vanished out of sight.
Wisdom returned to him, and with it tears,
The happy tears that heal the sorrowing heart,
Submissive to the ordinance of Heaven,
Content to live and die like other men.

THE LEGEND OF FREY BERNARDO.

THREE hundred years ago, or more,
In Portugal, at Santarem,
Between whose walls the Tagus flows,
Washing with lazy waves the shore,
A stately monastery rose,
Begirt with palaces, for there
The King in summer did repair
With his light loves, of course for prayer,
For their confessors came with them!
A busy place; for in the streets,
Where one to-day the muleteer meets,
Jogging in dust with jangling bells,
Rude as the mountains where he dwells,
Grave merchants met, who fortunes drew
From world-old lands discovered new
Beyond the dark and dangerous seas
By followers of the Genoese;
These, and the crews their ships who manned,
Whose cheeks with tropic suns were tanned,

Who rolled their costly bales ashore
With songs like ocean's stormy roar.
A holy spot was Santarem,
Famed for its tall cathedral spires,
That caught the morning's earliest fires,
And for the chapels under them,
Peopled with priests and sandalled friars ;
Famed for its monastery more,
For where 'twas builded years before
The Virgin in a Vision shone,
A lady on a golden throne,
Who in her arms an Infant bore.
To mark the spot they builded there.
A monastery, large and fair,
Whose doors were open night and day,
Inviting all who passed that way
To enter freely, and to stay,
If when within its walls they stood,
And saw its pious brotherhood,
The simple lives they led seemed good ;
As good they were to many then,
World-wearied, meditative men,
Who, till their spirits found release,
Desired forgetfulness and peace.
One of this sort one summer day,
Came to the monastery gate,
Burdened with some mysterious fate
That made him prematurely gray.
He may have been a banished lord,

Bereft of his ancestral state ;
A soldier who had sheathed his sword,
Repenting deeds of blood too late.
Whoe'er he was, he sought the prior,
And from that hour became a friar ;
Adopted all the brothers' ways,
And patterned after theirs his days ;
Rose when they rose at matin bell,
And went when they went to his cell.
Dead to the world, which missed him not,
But which he clung to with regret,
He struggled sternly to forget
Something that would not be forgot—
Struggled in silence and alone,
Asking no aid except his own
The spectre of his soul to lay ;
For he was never known to pray,
Either at morning's dewy prime,
Or Angelus, or vesper chime,
Though at the service of the dead
He closed his eyes, and bowed his head.
He lived not wholly understood
Among that simple brotherhood.
They pitied him for his distress,
That never sought relief in prayer,
But loved him for his gentleness,
And for the comfort he was there,
For many a weary heart and head
By him was sweetly comforted.

His was the hand, when they were ill,
And tossing on the bed of pain,
That gave the draught, and his the skill
That nursed them back to life again.
Such Frey Bernardo was, and so
The years with him did come and go,
Monotonous and dull and slow,
Till one dark day the pestilence
Broke out in Santarem, from whence,
Smitten with fear, the people fled,
Leaving the dying and the dead.
Then he arose in righteous ire,
Like one who has been calm too long,
And with quick steps, and eyes of fire,
And late-recovered manhood strong,
Went where the pestilence was worst,
And where they needed most his care,
Among the outcast and accursed,
Where death was in the tainted air :
He mitigated mortal pains
In cells where prisoners lay in chains,
And in the close dark hold of ships
Moistened the sailor's fevered lips :
Where the leech feared to go he went,
And to the sick and dying lent
Patience to live and strength to die,
And faith to pale priests standing by
To give them the last sacrament.
All man could do he did to save

His stricken fellows from the grave,
If ever doubtful, certain then
That God was served by serving men.
Before the pestilence was done
The shadows of departed lives
Filled all the streets of Santarem ;
Husbands lamented for their wives,
The widowed mother for her son,
And little children, left with none
To comfort or to care for them,
Wept for their parents up and down
That dark, depopulated town.
The heart of Frey Bernardo, wrung
At sights and sounds of sorrow, grew
Womanly o'er these waifs, who drew
Tears to his eyes, they were so young,
And so unfriended and alone ;
And two, whose mother he had known
In better days, and might have grown
To love, if fate had not denied,
And who—poor thing !—the hour she died,
Giving to each the parting kiss,
Had placed their little hands in his,
He fathered—he could do no less,
He pitied so their helplessness.
When the last sufferer was at rest,
And hushed the last, sad funeral knell,
He clasped the children to his breast
And bore them to his lonely cell.

Whether the saintly brotherhood,
To whom their cloistral solitude
And still, set ways alone seemed good,
Would let them stay with him, or he
Would have to shelter them elsewhere,
Troubled him at first, but needlessly,
The children were so welcome there.
What they to Frey Bernardo were
He could not, if he would, have told,
Nor how from his soul's sepulchre
The stone had suddenly been rolled,
And he had shuffled off at last
The stifling cerements of the Past.
But so it was. And he began
To put his old dead self away,
No more the lone and loveless man
Whose head and heart alike were gray:
For what a few short days before
Had pity been for their distress,
Had deepened into something more,
And now was anxious tenderness.
Sweet was the light in their young faces,
For the swift hours restored their bloom,
Unconscious of their childish graces
As dewy buds in secret places
Of their rathe beauty and perfume.
Perpetual sunshine filled his cell
Since he had fetched the children there,
And sweet, low voices, seldom still;

For long before the matin bell
Summoned the drowsy monks to prayer,
Before the earliest of the birds
Had piped its first, faint morning trill,
They wakened him with loving words.
He feared, in separating them
From all the children whom they knew
In their past life at Santarem,
He might, perhaps, have done them wrong
(And may have done so—who can tell ?),
There was so little he could do
To make them happy in his cell;
And shorten for them the long days.
They had a hundred little plays
That kept the days from being long.
Pablo, the youngest, had his toys,
Like other Lusitanian boys—
Rude images in clay and wood,
The Patriarchs here and Prophets stood,
With fishermen of Galilee ;
And there the followers of Mahound,
Their swarthy brows with turbans bound,
And red-cross knights, armed cap-a-pie.
If the girl, Inez, played with these,
It was to please her restless brother,
Who she had promised her dead mother
Should be her care when *she* was gone.
Left to herself, she sits alone,
Her small hands folded on her knees,

Holding her lately-counted beads,
Listening while Frey Bernardo reads
Black-letter tomes of ancient lore,
Which men, grown wiser, read no more.
Such was the quiet life they led
In the seclusion of his cell,
Through whose barred grate the sunlight fell
Till the hot sun was overhead ;
Then, wooed by softest airs and sounds,
They wandered out-of-doors together,
And flitting through the garden grounds,
Enjoyed the perfect summer weather.
Beneath the shady orchard trees,
Whose laden boughs with fruit were bent,
Hand locked in hand, the children went,
Their light locks fluttering in the breeze ;
The birds were singing far and near,
But they were hushed, content to hear
Such heavenly songs, so low, so clear !
What they to Frey Bernardo grew
As days went by, and their sweet ways
Became a portion of the days,
He rather felt at first than knew.
It was a pleasant sight to see
This grave, good man, erewhile so stern,
So gracious and so happy now ;
And how his loving eyes would turn
And watch the children, who had brought
Their brightness to his heart and thought,

The boy, say, sitting on his knee,
Where song or story he demands,
While closer still his sister stands,
Smoothing the furrows from his brow!
He told them stories such as he
Was told in childhood, and as we
Were in our later childhood told—
Old stories that are never old,
Despite their known antiquity;
For though mythologists may trace
Through all the lands their golden way,
Back to the cradle of the race,
They are as fresh and young to-day
As when they first were said, or sung—
Young as old Homer's song is young!
When these, which in his cell apart
Day after day the children heard
Till their light hearts no more were stirred,
For now they knew them all by heart,
Had lost their charm, he told them others,
As mythical, perhaps, as these,
Culled from the hagiologies,
Of holy fathers, sainted mothers,
Gone to their long and heavenly rest—
Only the sweetest and the best;
Not those that touched on martyrdom,
For soon enough their tears would come
For their own sorrows. "They shall be
Happy while they are with me."

Watching the pair with kindly eyes,
Which tears unshed would sometimes dim,
He pondered what they were to him,
And he to them—the tender ties
That bound their hearts together there,
Their confidence, his constant care ;
And pondering so one day his mind,
Which till that moment had been blind,
Saw what he had so long denied,
So dark had been his soul with pride—
The sovereign Fatherhood above,
The certainty of Heavenly Love !
"Thou art, whatever doth befall,
The Maker and the Lord of all ;
And as these children cling to me,
Hereafter I will cling to Thee,
Father and God." He said no more,
But wept he had not prayed before.

The legend ends here. But I know
It never ended here, nor so ;
For given the man whom I have sung,
Who was at once so old and young,
And who at last his duties learned
To God and Man—that man returned
Back to the world, where both could be
Much better served by such as he,
Who had begun by shunning them,
Than in his cell at Santarem.

THE BRAHMAN'S SON.

THE Brahman's son was dead, the Brahman's heart
Stricken as if a thunder-bolt had fallen
Out of a clear sky, emptied of all light,
And suddenly black with midnight. Nevermore
Would life be what it had been, for the hand
That, reaching from the darkness, plucked the flower,
Plucked up by the roots the stem that bore the flower,
And dashed it down to die the self-same death.
It seemed so, for the aged Brahman thrice
Fainted upon the bosom of his son,
And each time longer coming back to life,
Sank deeper deathward. When he lay as dead
They took the body from his lifeless arms,
And having washed it in the sacred stream,
And wound it in the perfumed linen sheet,
Laid it upon a bier bestrown with flowers,
And bore it softly to the burial place.
When, lying there, the unhappy father woke
He knew that all was over, for the tears,
That had refused to flow, began to fall,
As after a long drought the summer rain.
Moreover he saw the elders of his caste,
Gray-beards who had no children, rating him

Because he sorrowed for his dear, dead child.
Stunned by their harsh reproofs, that smote his ear,
With words of commination, he was mute.
Driven hither by his sorrow for his son,
And thither by his duty to the gods,
To whom all sorrow, save what they inflict
By priestly hands for gifts withheld from them,
Is sin, the Brahman sought to overcome
The dark remembrance of his dreadful loss
By brooding over the Beneficence
Which fills the world with light, the night with stars,
By wisdom which the wisest of his caste
Proclaimed the only happiness of man,
But sought in vain, for all day long he saw
The face, the form, the presence of his child.
Turn where he would it was : indoors and out ;
It went before him and it followed him,
Was at his scanty meals and at his prayers ;
Rose when he rose at morning from his sleep,
And in the troubled watches of the night
Was with him in his dreams—a beauteous shape.
Haunted by memories he could not escape,
And grief that would not heal, the Brahman sighed :
" I am not—cannot be—like other men,
For having their dead, as I have, they forget,
While I remember ; and not being wise—
No more than I am—they contrive to find

(They say so) wisdom, which I cannot find.
I will seek Yama, therefore, King of Death,
And pray him to give back my dear dead son."
The Brahman straightway rose, and clothed himself
In the long vestments of his priestly caste,
And having performed the ceremonial rite,
And offered up the sacrificial flowers,
Went forth alone to seek the King of Death.
He questioned all he met where he might find
That lord of vanished kingdoms. Where is Death?
Some stared at him wide-eyed, but answered not,
Thinking him mad; some answered, mocking him;
And other some advised him to return,
Lest, sooner than he would, he should find Death.
Scarred soldiers riding by in mail cried out
That Death was in the rush of battle-storms,
Beneath the bursting of the arrow-clouds,
Amidst the lightning of the crossing swords,
Before the ranks of fighting elephants.
And swarthy sailors, swaggering in their cups,
Boisterous as stormy sea-winds, shouted, "Death
Is in the long waves roaring on the reefs,
And in the water-spouts of the mid-sea."
And dancing girls, whose feet, like those of Spring,
Twinkled to music, and whose floating arms

Circled about their brows like flights of doves,
Sang, in the pauses of their amorous hymn,
"Not in the cold, dark caverns of the sea
Seek Death, nor in the dreadful battle-field,
But rather in our arms and on our lips,
Strained to our hearts in kisses: so to die—
No life is half so sweet as such a death."
The rippling laughter of the merry girls
Was like the chime of bells on temple eaves
When winds of summer lip their silver tongues.
He wandered by the banks of many streams,
And in the shade of many city walls,
Until he came to the great wilderness
Below the holy Mountains of the East.
Dangerous the way was, for in forest paths
Were hooded serpents, pendent from the boughs,
With flickering, forked tongues; and, couchant near,
Leopards, the anger of whose cruel eyes
Flamed ominously through the jungle grass;
And, still more deadly, the enormous boa,
Whose tortuous passage through the furrowed weeds
Was like a boat's wake on the heaving sea.
Fearless he passed them: what had he to fear
From deaths like these who sought the King of Death?
At length he reached the harmless hermitage
Where dwelt the oldest Brahmans—holy men,

Reverend in their white hairs and drifts of beard.
The shadows of the ancient rocks and trees
Lengthened and shortened with the slow-paced
hours,
And circled with the circling of the sun ;
All, save the shadow of the sacred trees
Wherein they sat and mused, which circled not,
Steadfast as earth was in the shifting light.
They sat in silence, staring at the sun,
Not blinded by it, and the birds of heaven,
Seeing they stirred not, nestled in their beards.
Awed by the stern composure of their looks,
The Brahman stopped, like one who in a dream
Fears to go on, yet feels he must go on.
Then, bowing lowly to these holy men,
He said : "O Brahmans ! Fathers of the caste,
As Brahma is the Father of the Gods,
Supreme in wisdom as the Gods are, hear,
And, hearing, help a most unhappy man
Who, worn with fruitless wanderings to and fro
In search of Yama, rajah of the dead,
Beseeches ye to tell him where he is :
Direct him, Fathers, to the King of Death."
He spake, and waiting for their answer, heard
The humming of innumerable bees,
The inarticulate whisper of the leaves,
The rivers chanting their eternal song,
And in the distant woods the roar of beasts.
But now the Brahmans heard, or seemed to hear,

Like those whom voices overtake in sleep,
And, who, persuaded by the voices, wake,
Not knowing where they are, or who they are,
Pausing until their souls come back to them.
"What man art thou? And wherefore seekest thou
Yama, who comes unsought to every man?"
Few words sufficed to tell them what he was:
A Brahman (as they saw), but one to whom
The wisdom of his caste had not been given,
Though he had sought it long, with all his mind—
Sought it with fasts and prayers for threescore years.
Seeing (he said) that he was growing old,
And was not growing wise—a simple man
Who never could be wiser than he was—
He took a wife, as was his duty then,
To bear him holy children; she bare one,
A son, who was the comfort of his age.
Him did he dedicate to holiness,
Instilling at all hours in his young life
The love of wisdom, teaching all he knew,
Till, no more teaching, he was taught himself,
Fathered in knowledge by his wiser child.
"But he was taken from me in his bloom,
Taken with the dawn of manhood on his lip,
Taken without warning, leaving me alone!
Wherefore, I pray ye, Fathers, holy men,
Who, knowing all things, know where Yama dwells,

Tell me where I may find the King of Death,
That I may pray him to give back my son."
They answered him together, with one voice,
As when the sounds of many swollen streams
Become one sound : "There is no giving back ;
Death takes his own, and keeps it; takes all
things.
The stars die in their courses, like the dew,
That shines, and is not ; the containing heavens
Wither like leaves in autumn ; all the worlds,
And all the creatures that inhabit them,
Vanish like smoke of incense—which they are,
From the beginning offered up to Death.
Thou canst not visit Yama's dread abode,
For no man goes that way with mortal feet.
But if thy faith be sure, thy courage high,
Thou mayst do one thing. Many a league from
here,
Hundreds of leagues toward the setting sun,
There is a valley ; in the midst of it
There stands a city, wherein dwells no man,
But the Gods only, when their pleasure is
To clothe themselves in shape, and live on earth.
There, when the eighth day of the month is come,
Comes Yama, from the dark realms of the dead,
To share the bright life of his brother Gods :
Go there, and there find Yama. Now depart :
We have heard and answered thy complaining
words,

And earned the right to meditate again."
Thus they, and silence followed, as when day
Dies in the purple west the birds fly home,
Forgetful of the songs they sang at dawn;
The leaves are hushed, the winds are laid, and night
Shuts suddenly, darkly in the starless sky.
Through sunlight, moonlight, starlight, like a cloud,
Driven by the strong wings of a steady wind
Whose speed is in his steps, the Brahman went
Hundreds of leagues toward the setting sun:
At last he reached the end of the world, and saw
The valley whereof the Fathers had foretold,
Immeasurable, and in the midst of it
The great and glorious City of the Gods.
A City builded in the summer clouds
By masonry of winds, fantastic, strange;
Tier over tier, in mountain terraces,
Sheer from the hollows of that happy vale,
It rose resplendent; leagues of palaces,
The sudden opening of whose doors disclosed
The light of thrones within; what temples seemed,
Interminable columns, crowned with domes;
Towers, wall-surrounded, high, mysterious;
Arches, wherethrough one saw the rise and fall
Of dazzling fountains in perpetual bloom;
Towers, temples, palaces, and over all
The great gate of the Palace of the Gods.

Beside the fiery pillars of this gate,
With folded wings, two watchful Spirits stood,
Guarding the entrance lest some evil thing
Should unperceived steal in ; who, when they saw
The Brahman coming where his prayers had come
So long before him—for the prayers of men
Are ladders mounting from the earth to heaven—
They knew his life had been acceptable
To the high gods ; and though he was the first
Who, without dying, ever came that way,
They stayed him not, such fearlessness of death
Was in his eyes, such certainty of life.
As when at set of sun on summer eves
The heavens are opened, and a single cloud,
Rising above the threshold of the west,
Pauses a moment, then is lost in light,
So paused the Brahman, till the golden gate
Unfolding slowly with melodious song—
If song it was, and not the spiritual touch
Of unseen hands on unknown instruments
That welcomed him—admitted him beyond,
There, where the Gods were in divine repose.
Not as where sculptured in colossal forms,
With fourfold faces, and with sceptred hands,
They sit crossed-legged, among their worship-
pers,
In tall pagodas, or in temple-caves
Quarried in mountains, ancient as themselves,
But Presences wherein the Power they were

Was felt, not seen : a sense of awfulness
Fell on the Brahman's soul, and closed his lips,
That would have uttered supplicating cries
To have his son restored, but dared not there.
From out the silence of that sacred Place—
But whether nigh at hand or far away,
From the great roof of brightness overhead
Or from the cavernous darkness in whose depths
The firm foundation of that world was set
From the beginning, who may say ?—there came,
Or seemed to come, a low mysterious Voice :
" Thy prayers are answered. All the Gods can do
For man is done when they have heard his prayers
And answered them ; the consequence of prayer,
Or good, or evil, must be borne by man :
The Gods are powerless to undo their work.
Thy son is in the Garden of the East.
Go to him ; I permit it." And he went,
Following he knew not how that heavenly Voice,
Sweeter than music on the sea at night,
But sadder than the moaning of the sea
When, pitying, it gives back the dead—too late!
Lovelier than all the gardens of the earth
It was—a region of eternal bloom :
Of flowers that, budding or full blown, were fresh
With lucent dews, whose bright leaves faded not,
Of fruits that, ripening on the laden boughs,

Dropped not, but hung all golden in the sun,
If sun it was whose mellow light was there—
An everlasting day! Like one in dreams,
Who bears about with him in unknown worlds
Remembrance of the only world he knows,
The unhappy Brahman wandered up and down,
Through groves of summer boscage blithe with birds,
And meadow hollows murmurous with bees;
Past sheets of still, clear water, islanded
With lily-pods—a Lotus Paradise,
And shafts of fountains flashing as they rose
In rainbow mists; past all, and saw them—
Saw nothing but his poor forsaken home
Beside the Ganges, and the mound of earth
That covered his dead boy, until, at last
The film passed from him, and he saw the boy,
More beauteous than on earth, though beauteous there,
Divinely fair—the same, but not the same.
Trembling, with outstretched hands, and a great cry,
He ran to him, and clasped him in his arms.
"Oh, my sweet boy! Oh, my beloved first-born!
Hast thou forgot me, thy father? me,
Whose loving heart was broken at thy death?"
"I know thee not," the soul of the dead child
Replied, escaping from his arms like mist.
"My son! my son! hast thou indeed forgot

Thy father, who loved thee more than his own
life ?
Who taught thy baby lips the words of prayer—
Deliverance from the power of Evil Ones,
And thanks for the protection of the Gods ?
Hast thou forgot thy mother, who, like me,
Weeps, but alone, seeing that I am gone
From her on this long journey after thee ?
O look at me ! O come to me again !
And look at me, and thou wilt know me ! " Still
The child came not, but said : " I know thee not :
Thou art a stranger to me. All I know
Is—that thou art a mortal, and not wise,
For wert thou wise, as we are, thou wouldst know
That 'father,' 'mother,' here are foolish names,
Belonging to conditions that are past.
Depart, unhappy one ! I know thee not.
Thou art no more to me than to the moon
The wind that drives the clouds across her face,
The torch gone out at noonday. Get thee hence ;
It profits not to bring thy sorrow here."
The child, the garden—all things disappeared ;
All save the Brahman, and the tears he shed :
Not long ; for lifting up his eyes, he saw
Buddha before him, seated on his throne,
Godlike and human, merciful and wise,
With eyes that read the secrets of all hearts.
Pitying the father who had lost his child,
He stooped and laid his hand upon his heart,

And healing his long heart-ache, gave him peace.
"Brahman! thou hast been punished grievously
For understanding neither life nor death;
For knowing not the spirits of the dead
Receive new bodies after they are dead,
So that their late-left tenements of clay
Are no more to them than a wayside inn
To which as guests they never go again.
The ties of kindred—father, mother, child—
That seem to bind the world with bands of steel,
Are frailer when death comes than spiders' threads;
For death comes like a torrent from the hills,
Which swollen with ruin sweeps away all love,
And all love clings to with its dying hold.
Thy first, last duty, Brahman, is to live,
True to thyself and others; swerving not
From what the voice within pronounces good.
Who lives well, dies well." So the Brahman found,
For he returned to earth, and wept no more;
But taking up the burden of his life,
He lived it out, and earned a quiet grave;
The thought of which, as he drew near to it,
Was a prophetic promise of his rest,
And of his bright Companion gone before,
Of whom his last words were—He knows me now!

THE LION'S CUB.

ONCE on a time there was an Indian King,
Dushmanta, who being young, and quick to love,
Youth's strength, or weakness, wedded in hot haste
A Brahman's daughter, in a holy grove,
Whereof she was the priestess. She was fair
As the white Ganges blossom whose pure leaves
Are woven of moonbeams ; fair she was, and sweet
As the first tender jasmin whose rare scent
Persuades the distant bee to seek it out,
And hoard its honey in his hidden hive,
But shy withal as the young antelope,
That in the sacred precincts of this wood
Fled from all steps, save only those that fell
From her light feet. Such was Sacontala,
To whom the great Dushmanta, King of Ind,
Smitten with passion, did espouse himself.
This is the prologue of a tragedy,
Which the strong hand that wrote a Winter's Tale
Might well have written, called The Fatal Ring.
The product of a Sanskrit poet's pen,
It turns upon the short-lived happiness
Of this mismated pair, who might have known,

At least, the man, as elder, should have known,
That, unless wife and husband be at one,
Of the same station, whether high or low,
Of the same race, alike in heart and brain,
The ring of marriage is a fatal ring.
So to Dushmanta and Sacontala
It proved before the crescent of the moon
Thrice rounding reached the full; above their couch
It rose, and shone, and set, till one dark night
Dushmanta came not; when it rose again
It shone upon Sacontala alone,
Deserted wife, who wet her couch with tears.
Wherein she failed to hold the man she loved
She knew not. Neither man nor woman knows
Why love, which comes and goes at its own will,
Once gone, like his, refuses to return.
She may have been too humble, he too proud;
For there is that in kings which makes them set
A greater value on the things they give
Than on the richer treasure they receive.

At length her father, who was old and wise,
Seeing Dushmanta never sent for her,
Nor ever came to their still hermitage,
Determined, after meditating long,
To send her to her lord, which was not wise;
But she, true woman and true wife to him,
Though by his strange desertion hurt to death,

Proud where she was once humble, liked it not,
And, following her own counsel, which was wise,
Would not have sought, nor seen him till the hour
When he, unkind no longer, should return,
And say, "Forgive me, dear Sacontala."
Yet being obedient, as daughters were
In that old time and that far land, she went
Whither her father sent her, loth to leave
Her half-sheathed lilies, and her unseen bird,
And the coy antelope, that, bolder grown,
Would have gone with her out of that close shade,
Into the great, bright, noisy, unknown world.

Veiled, as became a young and modest bride,
But clad in a rich mantle, such as Spring
Wears when in mid-May blooms men stop and say,
"Spring will be Summer soon," Sacontala,
By two grave Brahmans led, her father's sons,
Began her journey, which, through groves of palms
That fringed the roadway, and through millet-fields
Where busy husbandmen were sowing seed,
Past bamboo huts where children were at play,
Stone temples, where old priests were chanting hymns,

Pouring libations to the bounteous gods,
Led to the stately city of her lord,
Which, in its golden splendor seen afar,
Like the beclouded but uprising sun,
Reaching, they enter by the eastern gate.
A glorious city, into whose broad streets
They passed, Sacontala with timid steps ;
For, faint with travel and a heavy heart,
Bearing a secret burden in her breast,
She faltered ; but her Brahman guards were firm,
Not comprehending why she suffered so,
Austere as in the rustic solitude,
Where, meditating on morality,
Their studious but unfruitful years were spent.
So into and along the spacious streets
Swarming all day with jostling life they went,
Past booths and markets gay with fruit and flowers,
The shops where native workmen wrought in gold,
Setting of jewels, diamonds, Ormuz pearls,
Bazars where foreign merchants showed their stuffs,
Silks, satins, woven in barbaric looms,
The lordly pleasure-houses of great lords,
The palaces of princes, on, and on,
Till, last, they gained the palace of the king.
Silently entering through more silent guards,
Armed with tall bows, tough shields, and horrent spears,

Through long-arched chambers, where priests
murmured prayers,
To where, like Brahma on his judgment-seat,
Whither all might come at all times, and demand
Justice, or mercy, boons of life and death,
Surrounded with his glory, sate the king.

What passed between Dushmanta sitting there,
And his forsaken queen, Sacontala,
Our Sanskrit poet in his tragedy
Paints with pathetic force in simple words,
Which my best English fails to reproduce,
So poor my craft beside his perfect art.
An undercurrent of enchantment runs
Through his sweet scenes, wherein Sacontala,
While dipping water from a woodland stream
To quench her thirst, cup-wise, in her white
hands,
Dropped her betrothal ring, whereby she lost,
Her husband's love—but that was lost before.
For, disappointed from the first, he found
The ring of marriage was a fatal ring.

They met, and parted, not as king and queen,
But rather as lesser people meet and part,
Who, when estranged, as they were, separate,
Each picking up the broken thread of life ;
Women, their daily, narrow household tasks,
And men the broader duties of mankind.

The Lion's Cub.

Like one who, gliding in a soft, sweet sleep,
Past shores of summer rest he wots not of,
Reaches the happy world of heavenly dreams,
Whose only lord is love—to find love dead,
With no remembrance of his perished power,
Not even the ashes in his broken urn—
Such was Dushmanta's desolated heart.
Oh, what the soul of poor Sacontala?

Along the circuit of seven troubled years,
Wherethrough, like a fading Spring in silver mist,
There wavers the shadowy boscage of a wood,
Where mother-parrots in the pendulous nests
Feed their unfledged but ever clamorous young,
And where the vision of a woman is,
Clad in a roseate robe of woven bark,
Morning in her wan cheeks, and more than
 night
In the dark splendor of her drooping eyes,—
This past, we are in a forest, where we see
A child, but of no childly countenance,
Whom two pale women struggle to detain,
In vain, so hard his clutch upon their hands,
Playful, but powerful, as the lion's whelp,
Which, with torn mane, he haled a moment since
From the half-suckled nipple of a lioness.
"Open your jaws, that I may count your teeth,
Cowardly cub!" To whom one woman said:
"Intractable child, why dost thou so torment

The wild, young creatures of this hallowed spot,
As dear to us as Camadeva's doves.
Well have the Brahmans called you the all-tamer."

Here, like a presence stealing through the place,
The shadow of a ruler, unto whom
Life had grown lamentable since he lost—
What precious treasure had this monarch lost?
His dreams were of an unknown hermitage,
Where wandered an unknown woman, whom the bees
Honored like the honey in the lotus flower;
Here elephants that trampled trees, and there
Wild buffaloes wallowing in shallow pools;
A penitential voice that would be heard;
Kinghood abandoned, like the winter wind;
The supplicating trust that weighs down kings,
Who fail to rightly govern the sea-girt world,
On whom the sole support of all mankind
Rests like the largest of the Himalayas.
Then spoke Dushmanta: "Why is my fond heart
So drawn to him? He cannot be my son,
For I am childless, and my race is dead."

"The lioness will rend you like a reed,
If you do not let loose her tawny whelp."
"I fear her not." Whereat he bit his lip,
And glared defiance from his ireful eyes.
"A valorous child!" the brave Dushmanta said:

"Dear boy, release that royal prince." "Not
so."
Seizing the loose nape of the little lion,
The lad rose suddenly on his sturdy feet,
And cuffed the whimpering creature, right and
left.
"There are marks of empire in his baby palms,
And the round of sovranty is on his brow."
More had been said, had not the antelope
That browsed near by, in terror snapped its chain,
Welded of silver linked with costly stones,
And flown afar to lone Sacontala,
Its gentle mistress, gentler than itself.

Meantime, Dushmanta bent his stoutest bow,
Stringed with its arrowy lightnings, self-restrained,
Because the hour appointed was not come.
"Great love I bear this uncontrollable child
Who should be mine, but is not! Great would be
His inarticulate prattle and small laugh."
"Command him to set free the lion's cub."
"Why wilt thou, boy, dishonor thus thy sire?
Only the hooded snake with forked tongue
Infests the boughs of the odorous sandal-tree."
Whereat Dushmanta in his mighty grip
Caught the more mighty grasp of the boy's hand.
"Marvel of marvels!" "Why this outcry, pray?"
"Behold the curious likeness of this child
To thy most royal self, which not before

Hath bloomed with grace upon him." Here the king
Stooped his tall height, uplifting to his breast
The boy, and questioned him about his kin.

But now the fawn, no more alarmed, but brave
As the freed whelp, brought on Sacontala.
Wondering to find her husband standing there,
As in her joyous vision long ago,
And kneeling : " Forgive me, dear Sacontala,
Wronged as thou wert, and art, but not again,
For my right mind came back with the lost ring,
Found "—But we know how all lost rings are found,
From that of Gyges to the richer one
The Phrygian monarch dropped among the reeds,
That whispered his long secrets to the wind.
This late-recovered circlet was not now
An ominous but ever-fortunate ring,
So strong the triple love that bound the hearts
Of glad Sacontala and great Dushmanta,
And that young conqueror of the lion's cub.

THE END.

www.ingramcontent.com/pod-product-compliance
Lightning Source LLC
LaVergne TN
LVHW021404110826
845150LV00007B/1777

9781425512262